MORE BOOKS BY KATLYNN BROOKE

www.katlynnbrooke.com

The Six and the Crystals of Ialana, Book One of the Ialana Series

myBook.to/thesix

The Six and the Gardeners of Ialana, Book Two of the Ialana Series

myBook.to/thesixbook2

The Six and Anwyn of Ialana, Book Three of the Ialana Series

myBook.to/thesixbook3

The Tree Wizard of Ialana, Book Four of the Ialana Series

myBook.to/treewiz

Tea, Scones, and Malaria

Tea, Scones, and Malaria

A MEMOIR OF GROWING UP IN AFRICA

KATLYNN BROOKE

Tea, Scones, and Malaria is a work of nonfiction. Names and identifying details have been changed unless otherwise indicated.

First Edition March 2021

Photos are from the author's private collection.

Identifiers: ISBN: 978-0-578-87615-3

Publisher: KATLYNN BROOKE

www.katlynnbrooke.com

katlynn@katlynnbrooke.com

Edited by Cory Helms

Cover Design by Giraffe Light Media, Stephanie Katz

http://www.giraffelightmedia.com

Formatted by Dragon Realm Press

http://DragonRealmPress.com

To Mom and Dad, Ouma and Oupa, Butch, Rabbit, and Queenie.

"*Africa changes you forever, like nowhere on earth. Once you have been there, you will never be the same. But how do you begin to describe its magic to someone who has never felt it? How can you explain the fascination of this vast, dusty continent, whose oldest roads are elephant paths? Could it be because Africa is the place of all our beginnings, the cradle of mankind, where our species first stood upright on the savannahs of long ago?*"

—*Brian Jackman*

TABLE OF CONTENTS

INTRODUCTION

"When an elder is gone, a library burns to the ground"
— African proverb

Tea, Scones, and Malaria is a memoir of my life growing up in Rhodesia. It covers a period of twenty years, from my birth in 1950 through 1969. My focus is on the early years of my childhood and teens. The purpose is to offer the reader a glimpse into what it was like to live in Colonial Africa. This book is intended for American readers—those who know little about Africa and nothing about Rhodesia (which is now called Zimbabwe).

Why did I write this memoir? To answer some of the many questions I am constantly asked about my life in Africa, not the least of which is, "What did you eat?" This preoccupation with food suits me fine. I love food. African food is both amazingly delicious and horrifically disgusting to the uninitiated. I discuss food a lot. African food fuses native dishes with European and Asian cuisine. There is nothing quite like it in the rest of the world.

Another question that is frequently asked is "What is your ethnicity?" I identify as white European, but my genetic heritage is, like our food, an amalgamate of different races. My East African mtDNA is L0, belonging to the oldest race of humans on earth. Mitochondrial DNA can be traced back for a thousand years, or a dozen generations. Our oldest DNA is L0, from mitochondrial Eve (200,000—300,000 years ago). It is certain we all come from this originally, but it is interesting to know that my 6th grandmother, Barbara, was of this race. I suspect that she was a Khoe-San, a Cape local known as a "Hottentot," a woman from the bushman tribe like those featured in the South African movie of the 1970s, The Gods Must Be Crazy.

My genetic background is varied, ranging from mostly European to African, Indian, Arab, and Indonesian. All my non-European ancestors were slaves, brought to South Africa by the Dutch and Portuguese slave traders. They inter-married and bred with my French, Russian, Scandinavian, Dutch, English, Italian, and German forebears. Although my family settled in South Africa from the 1600s through the 20th century, my parents immigrated to Rhodesia in the 1940s, Mom as a missionary, Dad as a builder for the Rhodesian government.

Some think Zimbabwe may be a part of South Africa, but it never was a part of South Africa. Zimbabwe, formally known as Southern Rhodesia, was a British colony until 1965. It was and still is a separate country from its neighbor to the south. In 1953, it became a Federation with Northern Rhodesia (Zambia) and Nyasaland (Malawi) to the north. In 1965, the Prime Minister, Ian Smith, declared unilateral independence (UDI) from Britain, and the colony broke away. It wasn't until 1979, after a protracted civil war, that it achieved its independence as a majority rule country, and Rhodesia became Zimbabwe.

I left Rhodesia in 1970 and lived in South Africa until 1979 when I emigrated to the USA and became an American citizen in 1984. My parents were South African by birth, and they remained in Africa until their deaths. Many ex-pat

Rhodesians have a strong nostalgia and love for the country, mostly for what it used to be. They are known as the "When-we's." One can hold two truths in one's mind, simultaneously. While Rhodesia during the colonial period was a wonderful place for white people, the civil war that raged from 1964 – 1980 did not occur in a vacuum. The consequences of the systemic racial divide from the country's inception by colonialists who had no regard for the well-being of the local population were inevitable. The result is the basket-case that is now Zimbabwe. Fond memories are there, but so is the knowledge that native Africans were not on an equal footing with whites. The pendulum has swung to the other extreme, and now it is white farmers who are suffering under the majority rule.

The divide was, at its core, between black and white people, but it was also a power struggle between the two principal African tribes: the Matabele or Ndebele, and the Mashona (Shona) or Rozwi tribes. White people, mainly Europeans, settled the area that is now Zimbabwe in the 1890s, and Cecil John Rhodes (after whom the country was first named) created a new colony for Britain. At that time, the Mashona and Matabele tribes were the majority occupants of this territory. Their languages and cultures were vastly different from one another's, and there has always been tension between the tribes. Many indigenous Africans fought on the side of the white population during the civil war, hoping to end up on the right side of a power struggle. It would take several books to cover the history of this part of Africa.

Nothing is as simple as it sounds, but I try to convey in my memoir exactly how I perceived things from my limited perspective as a child. I write about the idyllic existence whites led—a feudal class system that excluded the native population. It can be compared to the racial inequities in the United States before 1970, a system similar to that of South Africa and its one-time system of Apartheid.

One cannot write about Zimbabwe without mentioning the natural, majestic beauty of the country, and the wildlife of the African savannah, the beautiful towns and cities, and the productive farms. However, the whites would not have been so lucky without the help of the native population in building an infrastructure and supplying the labor for the farms and cities.

In the 1950s, my family were pioneers who headed out into untamed areas far from towns or cities. My father's government job in construction took him, and us, into areas where there were few roads and little infrastructure. I grew up in this environment and became one with it. We ran wild and barefoot in the bushveld. Sometimes I feel it is a miracle we survived the harsh bush life at all. My life was not typical of most whites from this part of Africa, but I am sure there are many Zimbabweans who can relate since Zimbabwe is largely a rural land. Our life was much more primitive than most of those who lived on farms or in towns or cities.

For the first two or three years of my life, we lived in Bulawayo. Mom and Dad were heavily involved in church activities, and most of their friends were from the church they attended.

My grandparents, Ouma and Oupa (grandmother and grandfather in Afrikaans) also lived in Bulawayo, a few blocks from our first home. Originally from South Africa, their native tongue, Afrikaans, is a bastardization of Dutch, a mishmash of languages that reflects the true Afrikaner heritage — a racial mix.

Mom's father, Oupa, was a practicing alcoholic until the disease finally killed him with a series of debilitating strokes. Ouma, a classic enabler, took refuge in religion and her chronic neurosis. These days, she would probably be diagnosed with PTSD or depression. Mom told us many stories of growing up in this dysfunctional household. Her childhood only made her more determined never to touch alcohol, or to pass on that legacy.

This memoir is not written as a nostalgic trip down memory lane aimed at my fellow expats. There are plenty of those books already out there. My goal is to help readers who have never been to Africa, who know little to nothing about it, to gain a better understanding of the land and its people as they were at that time. I want those who read this memoir to feel what I felt, to see what I saw. I want the reader to gain a broader understanding of a lifestyle that was different and alien to most people of western civilization. I want people to understand how things were from my point of view, what we experienced — the splendid, the sorrowful, the atrocious, and the whimsical.

I have also written in a style and language that will be easily understood by non-expats. Africans of all races speak a lingo that can be confusing and only understood by those who have lived there. Since some native Africans did not speak English perfectly, such as our maid and nanny, Petina, I have allowed her authentic voice to come through. The rest of us speak the Queen's English, or American English, in most cases.

I have changed the names and descriptions of the people I knew and grew up with. Some characters are composites, and I doubt the people mentioned in this memoir would be recognizable to any person who knew me. I do not use real names for myself or my friends and family. Where names are real, I will indicate that at the time, but for the most part, the names are not the actual names. The people and events are real, however. I have tried as much as possible to recreate scenes and events as accurately as I am able to, but when it comes to remembered conversations, I must rely on how I felt at the time to convey the tone or spirit of the conversations. At times, I have recall of the exact words used, and those I've used as I remember them. Where I am too young to remember, I must depict the scene using artistic license, or, as it was told to me by my parents or grandparents.

Whatever you think of this memoir, I hope that above all else you will find it an enjoyable read!

Katlynn Brooke (aka "Pie")

ACKNOWLEDGMENTS

So many people have contributed to the creation of this memoir; I could never have written it in a vacuum. While my own memories make up the bulk of the writing, I have needed memory jogs, factual information, and help from those whose memories of the "good old days" are inexhaustible. These people include my sister, Kathy ("Queenie" in the book) and members of a Zimbabwe Facebook group who are a limitless resource for factoids and "how things used to be" when my own memory fails me.

I want to give a special thanks to Cory Helms, who edited the book. Her unparalleled skill and advice got me through the difficult parts. She has been a gift to me, and there aren't enough words to express my gratitude.

Without my Inklings writer's group, I would not have had the feedback necessary to constantly polish, rework, and improve upon the content. Their boundless patience, support, and advice over the months it took for me to write this memoir is appreciated more than words can say. Huge thanks to Aimee, Cory, Kim, Beth, Audra, and Bill.

Thank you to my Beta Readers—Karen Krieger, Pam Burch, and Pam Perkins. Your feedback and willingness to read an untested memoir is appreciated. Your comments are invaluable.

Last, but not least, my husband, Charles, who has made all this possible. He has supported me every step of the way. Thank you.

MAPS

A Map of

AFRICA

Rhodesia

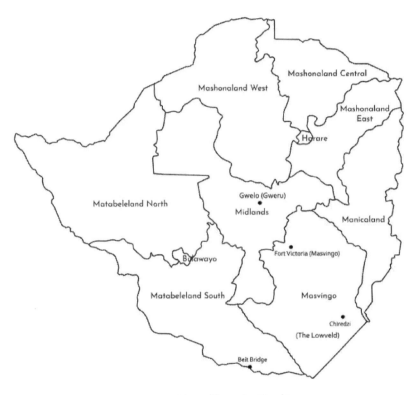

ZIMBABWE

GLOSSARY

- *Ag man* — (Rough "g" sound as in Ugh) An Afrikaans exclamation.

- *Armstrong-Siddeley* — A British luxury vehicle of the first half of the 20th century.

- *Bakkie* — (Buckee) A small pickup truck.

- *Beano* — A British comic book for children.

- *Bilharzia* — (Bill-har-zee-uh) A parasitic disease found in water.

- *Biltong* — (Bill-tong) Dried beef jerky.

- *Boerewors* — (Boo-ruh-vors) An Afrikaner sausage.

- *Bokvleis* — (Bok-flays) Goat meat.

- *Braai* — (BrI, I as in "eye") An African barbeque.

- *Cerveza* — (Ser-vay-zah) Portuguese for beer.

- *Chikwambo* — (Chick-wam-bo) See Tokoloshe.

- *Consul* — A British-made car.

- *Dagga* — Cannabis, marijuana (Dag-ah. The "g" sound is in the back of the throat, like the German "ch," only rougher).

- *Fanegalo* — (Funny-gah-law) A pigeon mix of African languages with English.

- *Guti* — (Goo-tee) A soft, mist-like rain.

- *Kaross* — (Kah-ross) An animal skin blanket used by the Khoikhoi of South Africa.

- *Koeksisters* — (Cook-sister) An Afrikaner pastry deep fried and drenched in syrup.

- *Kopje* — (Kop-ee) A small, rocky hill.

- *Lorry* — A truck.

- *Makiwa* — (Muh-kee-wha) Shona word for white people.

- *Miombo* — (Mee-om-bo) The Miombo woodland is found in tropical and subtropical grasslands, savannas, and shrublands biome.

- *Mopane* worms — (Mo-pah-nee) A caterpillar that feeds on the mopane tree leaf. An African delicacy.

- *Mozzie* — Slang for mosquito.

- *Muti* — (Moo-tee) African medicine.

- *Nganga* — (In-gung-gah) A healer, witchdoctor, or diviner.

- *Ngozi* — (In-goh-zee) Avenging spirits of the dead, Shona.

- *Nzou* — (In-zoo) Elephant in Shona.

- *Ouma* — (Oma) An Afrikaans name for grandmother.

- *Oupa* — (Opa) An Afrikaans name for grandfather.

- *Padkos* — (Pud-kos) Road food.

- *Paraffin* — Kerosene.

- *Piri-Piri* — (Pee-ree-pee-ree) An African chili.

- *Rondavel* — (Ron-dah-vel) Round hut with thatch roof.

- *Sadza* — (Sud-zuh) Cornmeal mush, a thick porridge made from mealie-meal/cornmeal.

- *Shave* — (Shah-vee) A wandering spirit in Shona belief.

- *Shumba* — (Shoom-ba) Lion in Shona language, or slang for "Lion Beer."

- *Stompie* — (Stomp-ee) Slang for a cigarette butt.

- *Tickey* — A small coin worth three pennies.

- *Tokoroshe* (alt. Tokoloshe) or Chikwambo — (Tawk-uh-loshee) (Chick-whum-bo) A sprite; a dwarf-like creature that causes mischief in the home or even illness and death.

- *Yebo* — (Yeah-baw) Shona exclamation to show approval.

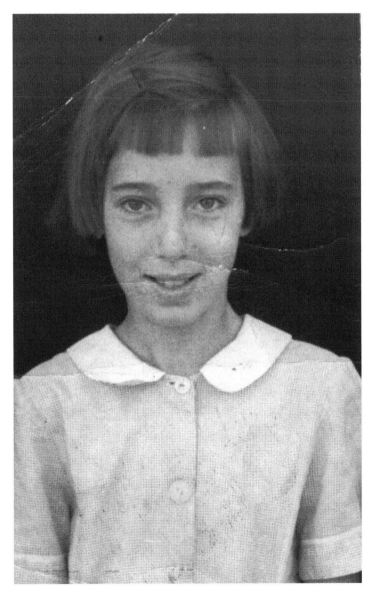

Pie, age 9

PART I

THE WILD CHILD

1950 — 1959

Tea, Scones, and Malaria

CHAPTER 1

MOM AND DAD

"Children learn more from what you are than what you teach them."

— Unknown

FORT VICTORIA, 1962

Like a leopard stalking a troop of preoccupied, garden-raiding baboons, Dad walks into the room while we are in the act of rifling through his bedside drawer. He points his stubby forefinger at us—the one that is missing its first digit, lost in an old carpentry accident. "I thought I told you to stay out of my stuff."

My mouth drops open, and the white-blonde head of my younger sister, Butch, swivels toward me. "It was Pie. She's looking for chocolates." Rabbit, my eight-year-old brother, stares up at the ceiling. *I have nothing to do with this either*, his eyes seem to say. Queenie, still too young to understand we're in trouble, giggles and points at me. "She did it!"

Dad's blue eyes alight on the thing I am holding in my hand. Instead of chocolates—I should have known better; Dad does not have Mom's sweet tooth—I am clutching a pelt of colorful feathers. I am a thief caught in the act. We are a family of chocoholics and behave like tweakers looking for our next fix, but Dad's weakness is salted peanuts. We have just discovered the brilliant pelt hidden under his stash. Dad reaches out, and I hand over the pelt. "Dining room," he says, jerking his head toward the door.

Dad smells of motor oil. His khaki shorts are stained with grease from the old Siddeley truck's gearbox that he has been working on all day, hoping it will be in running order by Monday. Mom is out shopping. My eleven-year-old brain told me we had a few minutes of freedom to go digging through their bedroom drawers. How wrong I was.

We gather around the tarnished but solid mahogany wood dining table. Petina's soft singing, a Shona lullaby, drifts through the kitchen door as she prepares our evening meal. Johnny, her baby, rests on her back, wrapped in a length of blue and white cotton. The occasional clatter of cups and saucers rises above the menacing but familiar hiss of our unreliable pressure cooker.

We — Butch, Rabbit, and me — settle into the dining room chairs' worn seats. Queenie is there too. She hates being left out of our affairs, even if it involves a "talking to," or worse, the belt. I sigh. *At least Dad didn't get the belt out.* The ripped green Naugahyde covers scratch my bare legs. I pick at a scab on my knee as I await the lecture to come.

Dad places the pelt on the table as he sits down. "Tea, Petina!" he yells, but Petina has already anticipated him. Her bare feet scuffing on the tile floor, she enters the dining room carrying a tea tray. Her baby Johnny gazes at us with round doe eyes from his kangaroo-like pouch. Placing the tray gently on the table, she scuffs out again. Dad lifts the beaded doily from the milk jug, pours a dollop of milk into his cup, then a heaping teaspoon of sugar. He waits a while, tilts the teapot, and a stream of dark liquid fills the cup to its brim. Petina knows how strong he likes his tea, and she never disappoints.

Sighing with satisfaction, Dad begins to sip. We wait. Tea is his pacifier, his soother of jangled nerves — of which lately, he has a jillion.

"This pelt is from a lilac-breasted roller," he says finally, placing the cup down and wiping his mouth with the back of his hand.

My eyes widen. I had guessed, though. The roller's pastel plumage, pinkish-lilac breast, and brilliant blue on its wings mark it as one of Africa's most beautiful birds.

"Listen carefully, because one day you may be in the same situation I was, and I want you to make the right choice."

We look at each other. This may not be as bad as we'd anticipated.

"It was just after I'd received my very first paycheck on the mines. I'd bought a rifle, and I couldn't wait to try it out. The man I bought it from promised me it would shoot straight, and I also wanted to see how my aim was. Shooting at unmoving targets seemed too tame. So, I went out into the bush to find something to shoot at. A splash of color in a tree drew my eye, and I lifted the rifle and took aim." Dad pauses for a moment, and, sadly, I think, looks down at the pelt, then takes another sip of tea. "I squeezed the trigger. To my surprise, the bird dropped with a small thud, like a stone. I walked over, picked it up, and stared at the dead thing lying motionless in my hand. Its eyes looked at me, empty of life and consciousness."

He looks up at us. "I thought I would be happy that my aim was so accurate, that I had hit my target, but I felt no joy in the act. I felt as if I had murdered the most amazing creature I had ever seen. This bird should have been alive, singing, making nests, and showing off its plumage; not lying lifeless in my hand." He lifts the pelt, shaking it slightly. "I kept this to remind me that we don't kill for sport. I kill so we can eat, not for pleasure. I get no enjoyment from killing a living creature." Placing the pelt gently back into the drawer, he turns. "Remember that."

Dad has hunted for a living. For many years he was forced to shoot meat for us and his workforce, to kill living things, but he tells us he gets no pleasure from it. To him, it is a necessity, not a sport. This is who my father is; his tough, he-man exterior hides a sensitive soul, but also one who can do the difficult thing when it becomes necessary. He can be frightening to us kids, using his belt on us at any infraction, but he only does it because he thinks it's the right thing to do. It's all he knows. Unlike Mom, who follows Dr. Spock like a religion, he knows nothing of the modern ways of child-rearing. His discipline is Victorian, and, thanks to his own upbringing, he finds it difficult to show that he loves us.

On the other hand, we have Mom.

Mom looks sideways at me as she sits in front of the old treadle Singer, while at the same time she expertly runs a seam. It is my school uniform, a blue and white gingham abomination that must be finished before Monday.

"You — Pie." Mom pauses, takes a breath, picks up a small pair of scissors, and snips the thread. Holding the nearly complete uniform up for inspection, she frowns. Her dark hair is graying prematurely, but her fine-featured porcelain face is still beautiful. "You are responsible for all of my gray hair."

"I know. You've said so before." I think a bit, frowning. Mom and I are kindred spirits, and since she's always busy with something, I value the little time we get to spend together. "So, why do you always call me Pie?" I ask. "It's not my real name. It's a stupid nickname. Why couldn't you choose something like…" my voice trails off. I can't think of what else I would prefer to be called. Princess, perhaps? Nope. I shake my head. That's dopey. A dog's name. I don't even like my real name. I wish it was something…something French, perhaps, like Charmaine, but it isn't.

"Because when you were born, I thought your face looked like a pie." Mom gives her trademark hyena bark. She finds this hilarious. I do not.

"And Rabbit? He doesn't look like a rabbit."

"He's quiet, like a rabbit."

"What about Butch?"

Mom's foot pumps the treadle again, her fingers flirting with the needle going up and down. She's already caught her thumb once in the needle, requiring a painful extraction and causing a swollen, bleeding thumb. "Dad gave her that name. She's a rough and tumble girl, and I think she wanted to be a boy. She acts like one. She used to catch spiders and eat them."

I shudder. "But…we both ate our poop!"

Mom nods and laughs again. "I was told by a psychiatrist that only creative kids do this. And you know how Queenie got her name."

"Yeah, she thinks she rules us all! She gets away with everything, especially with Dad. She's his favorite. But why do you always say it was me that gave you a gray hair?"

Mom puts aside her sewing for a while and folds her arms. "It was not only one gray hair. You have always been the most puzzling of all my children. You're not like your brother and sisters who give me very little trouble." Her smile, though, takes the sting out of the words. I have never doubted for a moment that Mom loves and values each one of us no matter what. I settle down to listen. Like Dad, her storytelling is often amusing, especially the tales about the things I got up to when I was still small, like…like…two years old. Or maybe four. Each time she tells them, I chortle as if I haven't heard the same anecdote a hundred times already.

"You won't remember that time you ate a whole bottle of baby aspirin," Mom says, "but I do, and it was only a miracle you survived."

"How old was I?"

"Eighteen months."

I nod, and as Mom speaks, early childhood memories begin to flood back. Rich, vivid cameos. Snippets of memories begging to be told. What I can't remember, my mind recreates in sound and images as if I do remember. But now, I don't know if it's my remembering or if it's what Mom has always told me.

I will start at the beginning.

Tea, Scones, and Malaria

CHAPTER 2

ASPIRIN, GERANIUMS, AND LIPSTICK

Pie and Butch, 1952

BULAWAYO, RHODESIA. 1950—1953

When Mom finds me, I am breathing rapidly, lethargic and unresponsive, on the bedroom floor, the empty bottle still clutched in my tiny hand. It has most likely only been minutes since I downed the last orange tablet, the contents of a full bottle of Junior Aspirin. I am eighteen months old, and my urge for oral exploration is still in its early stages. A door slams. It could have been Ouma as she runs over to our neighbor to use their

11

phone. Mom's ashen face looms over me as she lifts me from the floor, forces my mouth open, and sticks her finger down my throat, praying, beseeching God to save me.

At last, her efforts pay off. A gush of still-undigested pills, a torrent of orange lava, erupts from my mouth. It takes some time though before my breathing calms.

The doctor finally arrives, black bag and stethoscope in hand, but I have already emptied my stomach of all its contents. "You are lucky," he tells Mom and Ouma as he examines my vitals. "She ate too many, too fast, and they came back up again. I don't think there's any permanent damage."

I was born in 1950, at the height of the baby boom after WW2, the same year that Doris Lessing authored her first African novel, *The Grass is Singing*. Doris Lessing lived and grew up in my country of birth, Southern Rhodesia. She was familiar with Bulawayo, the city in which I was born.

From their marriage in 1949, Mom and Dad live in a southern suburb of Bulawayo. This area is old, with houses probably built just after the turn of the century.

Our tin-roofed bungalow has a long, wooden-floored, shot-gun style passage down its center, with rooms leading off on either side, and a large, airy wrap-around verandah. It sits in a good-sized yard surrounded by colorful, spicy pepper trees, tall, fragrant gum trees, and the ever-present pencil-tree cactus. This cactus emits a corrosive, milky sap when one snaps off a twig. Naturally, I do this often, and watch, fascinated, as the icky juice runs onto my hand. I think it's fairy milk. Our well-tended garden is fronted by a dirt road that leads to the main artery into the city.

Aloe, zebra plant, and sedum flourish in a rockery, and lantana, oleander, and bougainvillea shrubbery provide color to an otherwise drab landscape. Our climate tends to be on the dry side, especially during the winter. Hardy plants that take little maintenance are ubiquitous in this red-soiled area. A dusty, dry scent in the air reminds us we are not that far from the parched Kalahari Desert to the west.

When it does rain, I can't wait to run outside and sit in the greasy, red-brown puddles. I make mudpies, squishing the red soil through my fingers. I cover myself with the mud head to toe. It is my version of a spa treatment that once resulted in a temporary, itchy skin condition caused by miniscule soil parasites. Mom often sends me outside to play and, despite my track record, leaves me alone to do whatever my little heart desires. Mom, a firm believer in Dr. Spock, gives her children the freedom to explore.

I am easily bored, Mom is easily distracted, and perhaps she is also a slow learner. Dr. Spock has lulled her into a misguided trust of her first-born. True, she has a lot on her mind lately, with a toddler and a newly arrived baby. Around the age of eighteen months, my walking is that of a toddler's totter, but it's one that can get me far. One day, when Mom belatedly decides to check on me, I am gone. Frantically, she searches the house. Nothing. As she scours the garden, she glances up just in time to see a tiny figure making her way down toward the main road where we catch the bus into town. I am wearing a pair of her pointy-toed stiletto heels on each foot, an oversized purse clutched in a sticky hand. When Mom catches up with me, she notices I have also painted my face, like an ancient Barbarian in full warpaint, with her bright red lipstick that is so popular in this era.

"And just where do you think you're going?" She scoops me up into her arms. I can smell baby talc, and the faint gardenia of her favorite perfume, *White Shoulders*.

"To *townt*," I reply, drawing my brows together in a frown as if it were obvious.

Ouma, my grandmother, stands at the garden gate as Mom brings me back. She shakes her head, iron gray curls bobbing around a frowny face. "This child will be the death of me," she says, as she turns to go back inside. "I can't imagine what could have happened had she reached the bus stop."

Mom's laughter is a donkey bray. "I would have given anything to see the bus driver's face!"

Mom's benign neglect continues to have consequences, though. One particular day, Mom places me on a blanket on our usual spot on the verandah, alongside Butch, my baby sister. Ouma is visiting, helping her daughter indoors with something that does not include a toddler or a baby.

The verandah is a pleasant place. Red geraniums grow in pots that sit on the low, white-washed walls between concrete pillars. Potted ferns placed between the acacia-wood chairs with their colorful cotton print cushion seats lend a New

14

Orleans jazzy air to the polished red concrete floor's plainness. But it is the fragrant perfume of the geraniums, and their deep color, that fascinate me. *They look good enough to eat. What would they taste like?*

Getting bored with my toys, or perhaps wanting to be helpful, I decide, since Mom and Ouma are busy, and I have already sampled a petal, I will feed the baby. My two-year-old brain informs me that Mom will be pleased with my initiative. Reaching up to pluck the most delicate-looking geranium blooms, I enthusiastically stuff petals and leaves into the baby's mouth. Butch's arms wave feebly in protest, little legs kicking the air. She coughs and tries to spit out the strange matter, but I am not having any of that. More determined now, I shove the foliage in further. Butch's face turns a pleasing shade of purple, and she begins to gag. Indeed, I must be thinking, she will soon stop resisting and savor the crimson petals' subtle flavor, but her coughs only grow louder, turning, in a matter of seconds, into a crescendo of choking gasps.

When Mom and Ouma emerge, alerted to trouble on the verandah by the gagging noises Butch is making, the main suspect sits in one of the armchairs, clasping her hands in her lap.

"Kill that child!" Mom screams to Ouma as she frantically sticks her fingers down the baby's throat, scooping out leaves and petals as fast as she can. Ouma ignores Mom's directive, helping instead to excavate the debris from the baby's throat and restore her breathing. It is a successful rescue, and Butch lives so that her elder sister may torment her yet another day.

"You stared off into the middle distance," Mom tells me, years later. "Your face was so calm, as if you had no idea what you had done."

I am a tactile child, and I love color—red being particularly irresistible. My early training as an artist is launched during this stage of my life. One evening my parents are attending a dinner party hosted by Auntie Mary, Mom's cousin, and Mom unwisely makes a decision to take Butch and me along. Auntie Mary graciously offers her bedroom for us to sleep in while the adults dine.

"We've just had our bedroom painted," Auntie Mary proudly informs Mom as they tuck a blanket around me and my already sleeping sister. I am sure Mom also admonishes me to "be good," as she walks out the door to join the other guests. While I don't remember everything about that evening, I do remember the fresh-paint smell of the bedroom, and the mahogany dresser with its three-way mirror that sits next to the bed. It holds the usual accoutrements; a gold-handled hairbrush and a tray of assorted gold-colored objects. Some of them look familiar to me.

And isn't that a…?

The evening passes quickly for Mom, and soon it is time to collect the kids and put them in the car for the ride home. No doubt she feels a twinge of pride that we had been so quiet she had almost forgotten we were there. Mom and Dad thank the host and hostess for a wonderful evening as they make their way to the bedroom, grateful that, for once, they have been able to enjoy a rare, undisturbed night out.

As they open the bedroom door, the expression on my parents' faces is a picture of frozen dismay and horror. Instead of two sleeping children, one of them, their first-born, her pie-face shining with joy, adds the finishing touch to her masterpiece with a flourish. The remains of Auntie Mary's red lipstick, now an ugly stub in its gold applicator, is still in her hand. The walls, to a height of three feet or so, are covered in crimson squiggles, like a psychotic killer's insane ramblings written in blood at the crime scene.

It is most likely around this time of my life that Mom decides to allow Ouma more jurisdiction over my upbringing.

Tea, Scones, and Malaria

CHAPTER 3

OUMA AND OUPA

Oupa, hand on Butch's head; Ouma holding Rabbit, Pie in foreground.

1953, BULAWAYO

In 1953 I am an energetic three-year-old, and my sister Butch a two-year-old toddler. Mom is pregnant again, and in no condition to cope with my continued highjinks, so Ouma becomes my surrogate mother. I am the grandchild who spends the most time with Ouma and Oupa. I often stay with them in Bulawayo, and my memories are from an early age.

Their home is in the same suburb where we live the first years of my life. They share a large, single-family home divided into two apartments with the owner, Auntie Isabelle, living in the front part of the house, while Ouma and Oupa occupy a rear one-bedroom apartment.

Auntie Isabelle is an Afrikaner, a motherly, ancient woman with missing teeth and a shock of white hair, like Einstein. She loves it when I visit with her, and at age three, I am uncritical and open to all her misguided instruction. One hot day, I sit in her kitchen, watching a large spider on the wall, just above my head, catching and eating flies as if it is at a spider buffet. Auntie Isabelle places a bowl of porridge in front of me and hands me a spoon. Absentmindedly, I grasp the spoon with my left hand, my eyes still fixated on the spider as it pounces on yet another fat fly.

"No!" Auntie Isabelle exclaims, pulling the spoon away, then immediately handing it back to me again. Puzzled, I pull my eyes away from the wall and grasp the spoon, again. "I told you, *no*!" She jerks the spoon back.

I stare at her, the spider forgotten. She wants me to eat, doesn't she? What am I doing wrong? This goes on for some time. Finally, impatiently, she grabs my right hand, where it rests in my lap. "This one, child, this one!" It dawns on me that she thinks I am using the wrong hand, so, eager to please, I take a mouthful of porridge with the spoon in my right hand. It doesn't feel right, so I swap hands and am about to take another bite when a stinging slap on my left hand tells me this is the wrong thing to do. I am stubborn, but so is Auntie Isabelle. The slaps and the placing of the spoon into my right hand continue. I continue swapping the spoon back to my left hand until I've eaten my fill. I remain a southpaw.

Ouma and Oupa don't care which hand I use to eat — they turn me loose to sate my appetite in Auntie Isabelle's thriving orchard adjacent to the house.

"That kid must have a tapeworm," Ouma comments to Auntie Isabelle one day as they watch me down an apple, core and all. "I've never seen anyone so small eat so much."

"Like a goat," Auntie Isabelle sniffs, shaking her head. "And she still uses the Devil's hand."

The yard is divided in two sections, with an outhouse at the back that has full plumbing. It is a chore to walk down the long path to the outhouse at night, so we use the chamber pots Ouma always keeps under the bed. Behind the house is an apple orchard. Behind a fence, in front of the house, is yet another orchard of orange and lemon trees. The lemon trees bear jumbo-sized fruit with a thick, loose skin. The lemons and the skin are sweet and can be eaten like oranges. The orchard is redolent with the scent of orange blossom. At certain times of the year, we pick pomegranates from the pomegranate bushes. Eating pomegranates is a messy job that leaves us looking like victims of a massacre, but it remains my favorite fruit.

Near the front gate, under a pepper tree, is a chest-high red rock. How it came to be there, I will never know. It seems to me to be a meteor that had fallen out of the sky, or at the very least one of our enormous granite *kopjes* [a small rocky hill]. I clamber up it, daily, to survey the world. To me, this rock appears the size of the Rock of Gibraltar, and it becomes my ship, or whatever I want it to be. Years later, as I grow older and taller, this rock shrinks rapidly to the point where I can't even describe it as large anymore, just a weird rock that someone was too lazy to cart away. Strange how that happens.

Oupa's job is with Rhodesian Railways. Oupa, entrenched in his alcoholism, suffers a severe accident while on the job. He is a "shunter," an employee engaged on the ground with the task of having to get between the carriages to complete coupling and uncoupling. It is dangerous work at the best of times, but it seems he has also been drinking while on the job. He is pinned between two carriages, and it is only a miracle that he still lives. He spends months in the hospital, recovering, and never returns to work. Sometime in the Fifties he retires with his pension.

It becomes an ordeal with Oupa home all the time. He mumbles a lot and swears when he runs out of booze or cigarettes. He reeks of cheap Scotch and tobacco. He smokes the unfiltered Star cigarettes that he keeps in his front shirt pocket, reaching for the yellow pack with trembling, nicotine-stained fingers. Barefoot, I must dodge the still glowing *stompies*—butts—he flicks out into the yard when he's done. Ouma does not tolerate dirty ashtrays, although she does keep an abalone shell on the coffee table just for Oupa, but she empties it every five minutes. It annoys Oupa. Muttering, he rises from the rabbit-hide *kaross*-covered sofa and goes outside, taking his cigarettes with him.

Like his smokes, his raw cough is unfiltered; he hocks up something brown from the depths of his lungs, expelling it onto the sidewalk or driveway. I dodge those, too. Much of the time, I pretend Oupa isn't there, and that's not difficult, because he isn't—not the real man he had once been, the poet, writer, artist, and musician. The man I see now is a shadow of his former self, a *shave* [African spirit] who wanders around the property looking for cigarettes or his next drink.

I am often glad to see my parents pull up in the driveway, ready to take me home, away from the sickness and disharmony that are my grandparents.

Tea, Scones, and Malaria

CHAPTER 4

IRISH LACE

1953

om's days of apologizing for her eldest child are not over.

I am three years old, and this is one incident I remember quite clearly. We are visiting Dad's aunt Martha in Johannesburg. One does not call my great aunt "auntie." To Mom, she is formal and intimidating, a family member who keeps a spotless house. Her home looks as if certain areas need to be roped off, like a museum with valuable artifacts—a home where sticky-fingered children are not welcome. Aunt Martha has never had children. She doesn't like children, and I'm sure after this incident, she likes them even less, but what can Mom do except sit me down at the highly-polished mahogany dining room table with its upholstered dining chairs while she and Aunt Martha go into the kitchen to make tea. Mom doesn't forget the admonition to "be good," adding "don't move!" *There are surely no lipsticks here*, she must have been thinking, *so what trouble could Pie possibly get into?*

I have been told not to move, so I gaze instead at Aunt Martha's lace curtains that hang from the window behind the dining room table. They fascinate me. As an admiring Mom sat me down at the table, Aunt Martha declared that these are handmade Irish lace curtains that she had ordered all the way from Ireland. It doesn't matter to me where they come from. I agree with Aunt Martha. They are exquisite. I sit, bored, while my eyes trace the pattern: a scalloped edging that outlines a repeating design, row upon row of flowery clusters that run the length of the creamy curtains. The more I stare, the more I want these curtains. I want to wrap myself in them, drape them over my head like a bride, but how? They are attached to the window, but I need to examine the motif in more detail. I air-trace around the design with my finger. As I trace, my hand and eyes following each flower, leaf, or scallop, I frown. How can I engrave this in my mind, make it mine? I realize, from the clatter of cups and saucers, and the whistle of the kettle in the kitchen, I don't have much time left. It is then that I catch a metallic glint on the far side of the burnished tabletop. Mom has missed it entirely. A pair of scissors, beguiling in their keen, silvery promise, lies almost hidden under a lacy doily. Despite being told not to move, the compulsion is irresistible.

I reach for the scissors.

Mom and Aunt Martha return to the dining room, each holding a cup of tea in their hands. Standing on the table's mirrored surface, I have just finished cutting around the last ribbon of each repeating design in the lace. I am satisfied. I now understand the pattern, the design, and I will replicate it as soon as I have paper and crayon in hand.

"Pie!" Mom screams. Her face is as white as the tea cup she holds in her trembling hand. Tea slops over the cup's gold rim onto the shiny floor. Aunt Martha's mouth opens, then closes, and opens again. I think she must be terribly pleased with my initiative. So pleased, she is unable to speak. Unlike Mom, who has now found some words—words I cannot repeat here. I don't remember what happened after that, and perhaps that is a good thing.

Tea, Scones, and Malaria

CHAPTER 5

CORONATION

One of Mom's cakes. Left to right: Pie; our Nanny, Violetta; Rabbit and Butch

O ur sojourn in Bulawayo comes to an end. Dad insists his job can accommodate his family out in the *bundu* [bush]. Our gypsy life has begun.

Rabbit is born in May of 1953, and now we are a family of five. The Korean War has just ended. Joseph Stalin is dead. In Britain, King George died the previous year, leaving his daughter, Elizabeth, to take the royal reins in June.

As a three-year-old, I don't care about any of this when we move into our new home, a brick house in a tiny hamlet about 100 miles north of Bulawayo. Surrounded by bushveld and dry scrub on the Shangani River banks, it has some civilization pretense. We have neighbors, and there are other children I can play with.

This year, 1953, Britain has also created the Central African Federation consisting of Southern Rhodesia, Northern Rhodesia (now Zambia), and Nyasaland (Malawi). Mom and Dad are honored to be part of the colonial empire. Mom considers the royal family the last word in perfection. She has grown up with stories of Princess Elizabeth and her sister, Margaret, ensuring we are raised on stories of Elizabeth's daughter, Anne. I will be compared to Anne, frequently, and not in a good way. It doesn't take long before I begin to hate Anne. The biggest celebration of the year has arrived with Elizabeth's coronation as Queen of England.

Our neighbors have invited us to a huge bash, a coronation party, at their house. Mom has made me a new, red-ruched bathing suit, telling me that, now, finally, I can wear it since the children will be swimming in a plastic pool outside. For many days now I have been longing to put it on, but Mom says it's not suitable for everyday wear. We don't have a pool. Mom takes me into a bedroom and helps me change into my bathing suit. I have been eager to jump into the water on this warm day. I can hear the shouts and splashes of the children outside and the parakeet-like chattering of the adults who are congregating on the large screened-in verandah.

I finish changing, and Mom, hand on my back, ushers me onto the verandah toward the screen door that leads to a green and gold, sun-warmed yard outside. It is then that I hear gasps from behind me. Mom turns, and a long, admiring "Aaah!" escapes her lips. I turn my head. *What is the fuss all about? Do they love my new swimsuit as much as I do?* I quickly realize it is not my stunning appearance.

I slowly take my hand away from the door handle as my eyes follow the hostess who has just stepped out onto the verandah carrying a silver platter that holds—what? A crown? Plainly, I see now that she does not carry a real crown, but a cake that looks like one. The hostess places the tray onto a coffee table in the center of the room, and, pool forgotten, I stare, awed and envious, at this masterpiece of culinary art. I draw closer, sitting on my haunches next to the coffee table. I carefully observe every detail of the cake, the centerpiece of the party. *Oohs* and *aahs* ripple through the room as the adult guests gather around.

"I've never seen anything like it!" one guest exclaims.

"Where did you get all the glitter?" another asks.

"And the diamonds—can you eat them?"

"Oh, is that real velvet?"

"No dear, it's butter icing!"

I, too, want to ask all these questions, but no one pays any attention to the barefoot, dirty kid underfoot. I slide closer to better observe.

In the shape of a crown, the center, a "velvet" cap, sits under four fleurs-de-lis arches, each studded with edible jewels: diamonds, rubies, and pearls, topped by a *monde*—an orb—and a bejeweled Maltese Cross. The white frosting ermine trim at the bottom of the cake begs me to take my finger and scoop it, along with some of those glittering jewels, into my mouth.

I have never seen anything like this before. Mom's cakes resemble the brake discs from Dad's car, or an industrial project perhaps, and about as appetizing. She'd scrape the burned parts off, slap some apricot jam in between each layer, then cover the whole lopsided thing with gloppy butter icing. This cake is not one of Mom's. I want to hold it in my hands, pick off the rubies, diamonds, and emeralds and place them onto my tongue. I want to poke my finger into the velvety cap and discover what lies beneath. *Perhaps I can even put it on my head! Crown myself Queen!* The thought makes me quiver, giving me goosebumps. I sit on my hands in front of the cake, willing myself not to touch it. I am not interested in going out anymore. Instead, mouth open, I stare, my nose inches from this culinary splendor.

Timidly, I gather up the courage to ask the hostess if I could, perhaps, have a piece? Much like Oliver Twist holding out his bowl and asking if he can, *"please sir, have some more?"* The hostess bares her teeth at me. "Why aren't you outside with the other children?" She seems nervous. Mom has not noticed this exchange. She is talking to another guest, unaware of my interest in the cake.

The hostess, keeping one eye on the freckle-nosed kid sniffing at her prize, carefully removes the top decoration. It is the jewel-encrusted cross and orb. She picks up the silver cake knife that lies on the platter and plunges it into the cake. I watch as the blade slides down its center, slicing through creamy, rich blue icing and then into the ermine band. I bite my lip as she places the slice onto a delicate china plate, the moist, glistening, yellow sponge interior luring me ever closer with its sweet siren song. Our hostess smiles as she hands a slice to each guest, but I know, by her fixed smile when she catches sight of me still crouched near her prize, that if I make any move, she'll chop my hand off with the silver knife.

That day, not a single crumb of that cake, or its jewels, makes it anywhere near my mouth. The woman stands guard over it like a junkyard dog. It is a work of art that is much too good for kids. Instead, we children are served an inferior cake, one that, in my opinion, must have been donated by Mom. I glower at the sub-standard cake that sits on a small wooden table outside, being inspected by the family dog. The pink icing, as pink as the deworming medicine Mom gives us, is rapidly melting in the hot sun. The dog licks the cake, cautiously and experimentally. With a whimper, it shakes its head and trots off. The cake is lopsided, and besides the lick mark, someone has already stuck a finger into the icing. I know, without a doubt, it is Mom's cake.

Tea, Scones, and Malaria

CHAPTER 6

POPPIE

1953

I am a quiet child, and I get up to stuff. Bad stuff. Mom knows that only too well; this is where Ouma comes in handy. Oupa is of no use. He is not a typical, kindly grandfather who dotes on his grandchildren. I often get the impression he doesn't want us around since it interferes with his drinking. Ouma refuses to leave him, though. Instead, she makes many trips to South Africa to visit her family in the Cape.

She wants me to go with her.

Mom gratefully agrees, and we are dropped off at the Bulawayo train station, where we board the train. We share a sleeper compartment with a lady who reminds me of Olive Oyl in Popeye. Even at age three, I am familiar with Popeye. At home, Mom reads the Sunday paper comics to me, and Popeye is one of my favorites.

The lady who looks like Olive Oyl has twisted her long hair into a bun just above the nape of her neck and secured the whole thing on her head with a myriad of metal pins. She then fastens a spidery hairnet over the bun to ensure not a single hair escapes. My fingers itch to help, but to my disappointment, the request for my assistance never comes.

Instead, I watch, mesmerized, as she completes this process. I have always wanted to meet Olive Oyl in person. My wish has been granted.

I wish Ouma would grow her hair this long so I could help her put it up in a bun. Instead, Ouma's short, iron-gray hair frames her severe face with little rolls that she also pins into place. She calls these "victory rolls," but to me, they just look like dog poop. She wears cotton print dresses from the forties and sensible, lace-up shoes. Her only nod to femininity is the *Eau de Cologne* she douses herself with every day. It follows her around like a cloud wherever she goes. Her closets and clothes smell of lavender, and every time I get a whiff of lavender, I think of Ouma.

As the train chugs out of the station, Ouma unpacks our lunch for the next day.

"We're not using the dining car," she tells Olive Oyl. "I always bring *padkos* [road food]. I don't trust railway food." The woman nods but rises and leaves for the dining car. Ouma opens the sandwiches wrapped in tin foil, and the familiar odor of Marmite, a dark brown British culinary spread that looks like motor oil, hits my nose, along with the faint sulfur odor of the over-cooked boiled eggs that mingle with the compartment's coal dust and leather smell. Her eyes brighten as she pulls out two oranges and places them on the little table between the seats. "From Auntie Isabelle's trees!" She cuts them into small pieces with a knife she has in her kit. This is our padkos for the next twenty-four hours, which is how long a train trip to the Cape takes.

Our compartment is standard second class. The green leather seat's backrest lifts to a bunk-style bed, and the stow-away table where we are now sitting can be raised to reveal a small hand basin. After I finish eating, I pump the tiny faucet over and over so I can watch the trickling fountain of water that magically emerges from its spout. Ouma slaps my hand and tells me to stop, or she'll...the threat always remains unspoken.

I trace, with my finger, the ornate Gothic script etched into the window of the golden Rhodesian Railways logo. I open the window, sticking my head out to observe the steam locomotive pistons pumping away when we round curves. I open my mouth, my tongue out to taste the coal-soot that belches like dragon breath from the funnel. I pretend not to hear Ouma's frantic insistence that I get my head back in before a railway signal takes it off, and "Don't stick your arm out like that. You'll lose it when another train goes by!" I run up and down the narrow corridor outside our compartment, talking to all the passengers standing at a window gazing out at the monotonous, scrubby scenery.

As darkness descends and we've eaten the last of the sandwiches, Ouma turns on a little overhead lamp. Its warm glow is comforting, but I am no longer able to see outside. I am bored. I lie on the seat, kicking my feet against the side of the compartment. *Bam, bam, bam.* She slaps my leg. "Sit up, behave yourself, and I'll tell you a story."

Miss Oyl's eyes widen, as if she is the one who is bored. "Yes, please do! Tell me about your home. I believe you're going to visit your father?"

"Yes. My mother died years ago. Poppie's alone on the farm now."

"What does he farm?"

"Ostriches. Or at least he once did. There aren't any ostriches left on the farm now, though. There's no longer any market for their feathers. When I was a girl, ostriches were prized for their showy plumage, which, at that time, decorated rich ladies' hats worldwide." Ouma stared out the window as she spoke, even though she couldn't see anything there except for our ghostly reflections staring back.

"As the eldest child of seven children, it was my job to take care of the ostriches. One day, while I tended to the birds, I got too close, and one of them kicked me in the back. A kick from an ostrich can kill a man, so it is only a miracle I survived this, but I've suffered terrible back pain for years."

Miss Oyl gasps, her hand flying to her mouth. "Oh, you poor thing. What a hard life it must have been!"

"That's nothing," Ouma continues, her green eyes seeming to focus on a far-away time and place. "In 1900 I was seven years old. Poppie had gone to fight with the Boers against the English in the second Boer War. It was only me left on the farm, with Ma, who was about to give birth to my youngest brother, Albert. The only others who were there were the midwife, and my younger brothers and sisters. We had just been told the British were coming."

Her hand rests on her heart, as if to cover the fear she still harbors from that day. "We were told they would burn the farm and kill or imprison us. They had done it to other farms.

At that time, we, Afrikaner women and children, were often captured and taken to POW camps by the British soldiers, where we died of disease and starvation. I piled up all the furniture in front of the bedroom door, even though my back hurt terribly. Ma was screaming because she was about to give birth. We were all terrified. I had to do what I could to save our family." She sighs, pressing her lips together in a familiar Ouma scowl before continuing. "Luckily, though, the British never came. We survived the war, and Poppie returned home safely."

Ouma turns to look at me. "Now, it's time for you to go to sleep." I insist on sleeping on the top bunk, with my nose pressed against the window glass. It is dark outside, but every now and then, the roar of a passing train startles me awake, and mysterious lights whizz by. I wonder about the people standing on lonely platforms as we pull into a station. *Who are they, and where are they going? Are there ostrich farms out there? I really want to see an ostrich.* The clickety-clack of the wheels on the tracks finally lull me back to sleep.

I don't remember where we get off the train. It could be Port Elizabeth, the nearest city to Poppie's farm. Ouma reassures Miss Oyl, who is concerned we'll be stranded.

"Uncle Koosie, my brother, will come and get us." Sure enough, a tall man with a fedora pulled low over his sunburned face—Uncle Koosie—greets us on the platform. He drives us to our final destination, a town called Willowmore. I can't understand a word he says. He and Ouma chatter away in Afrikaans, and I am left silently sitting on Ouma's lap, admiring the scenery. The sparkling, sapphire-blue Indian Ocean disappears behind hills that slowly change to a dusty brown semi-desert of the Greater Karoo in the Eastern Cape. Poppie's farm is nestled in a small valley with the Swartberg Mountains as their backdrop. Despite the beauty of the setting, the ambiance remains melancholy and depressing. The mountains surrounding the small valley rise behind the farmhouse in a blue-gray backdrop. Fynbos, an evergreen, heather-like shrub, flourishes in the gravelly soil, and behind the house, a mountain stream burbles. I can smell the pungent, bushy fynbos, its peppery aroma making me wrinkle my nose like a rabbit. Orange and red aloes that look like red-hot pokers are the only color in a dreary, flinty garden that grows more rocks than flowers.

The farmhouse reminds me of our home in Bulawayo; a low bungalow with a rusty tin roof and a verandah that runs the length of the house. The interior is dark and forbidding, filled with clunky, old-fashioned furniture that looks as if it hasn't been updated since the first Boer War in 1880.

Ouma's mother had died before I was born, so it is only my great-grandfather in the big house and a live-in maid who has a daughter, Maisie, the same age as me. She and I play in the mountain stream. Maisie speaks Afrikaans, and I speak English, but we seem to understand each other well. Despite the resentment Ouma must feel toward anything English, she has raised her children to speak English as their first language. "You can get further in life speaking English," she would say. "Hardly anyone outside of South Africa speaks Afrikaans." Ouma spoke Dutch before she spoke Afrikaans. "When I was a child, we had a Scottish tutor," Ouma tells me as we sit on the farmhouse verandah. "In those days the farm did well with the ostriches, and Poppie could afford a tutor for us. We all learned to speak English from *our* Scotsman."

In later years, I pore over old photos of my grandmother and her siblings, standing amongst the aloes in the garden in their Edwardian clothing. She looks so different, her hair long and braided, her eyes staring into the camera with a hopeful, anticipatory gaze, one that does not yet know how much her life is destined to be difficult.

Poppie is intimidating. At first, his loud voice and barking laugh causes me to retreat. I peer out at him from behind Ouma's skirt, wondering if this old man is dangerous. I sense too, by her uncharacteristic submissive demeanor, Ouma is intimidated by him. (Years later, she tells me he had beaten her, using a leather-hide *sjambok* [a whip], the day before her wedding because she talked back to him.) He is a flinty old man, and his strident voice reverberates through the house. After a few days of being in Poppie's presence, I become accustomed to his bellicosity. I find myself sitting on his lap, laughing at his jokes, and wishing he would come home with us.

To Ouma's shock, he teaches me bawdy ditties in Afrikaans. I repeat them back, shouting them out, proud of my ability to now speak two languages.

"Ouma en Oupa sit op die stoep,

Oupa gee 'n harde poep.

Ouma se, 'Wat maker,'

Oupa se, 'My maag is seer!'"

The English translation does not do it justice. Ouma points out that Poppie prefers the alternate, more risqué, version of this ditty. Poppie's version loosely translated is:

Ouma and Oupa sit on the verandah.

Oupa farts.

Ouma asks, "What's the matter?"

Oupa says, "My stomach hurts."

In the more polite version, Oupa does not fart. He calls out, no doubt, in anguish over his digestive issues. I do not understand the meaning of the words. I repeat them, parrot-like, and Poppie's bellowing laughter echoes through the house. *"Again!"* he yells, slapping his knee. *"Again!"* And obligingly, in my little sing-song voice, I shout it out once more. Ouma's tut-tutting and head shaking does nothing to prevent him from teaching me even more verses, which, perhaps fortunately, I don't remember.

The main meal is eaten in the evening around a long wooden table. Poppie sits at the head. I remember more great-uncles and aunts visiting while we are here. They sit, mostly silent, at the table, while Poppie dominates the conversation. He loves to tease me about what I am eating.

"So, how do you like the *bokvleis*, eh?" he asks, his eyes sparkling with devilish amusement, as if he knows something about it that I don't. *What is bokvleis?* I wonder. I don't really care—the stringy goatmeat stew is delicious if somewhat gamey, but I eat it down as if it's roast sirloin. It comes as no surprise that Ouma never learned to cook, having grown up with this fare.

Poppie seems to be everywhere at once, his effervescent spirit demanding to be heard. He is a life-long member of the Dutch Reformed Church, and he reads passages to us every night out of his Dutch Bible passed down from generations ago. Poppie is also a flat-earther. He opens his Bible, his finger jabbing to the place where it says that the earth stands on four pillars. That settles it for him, and, when I think about it, for me too. I never could understand how the land we stood on could not be supported by something. I think the sky is a dome with little lights that come on at night. It makes sense to me. Ouma understands the science, though. She opines under her breath that the earth is round, but she never argues with Poppie. Her history with her father has been formed in a harsh Victorian era, when children did not speak back and were seen, not heard.

We have nightly prayers in the living room. We kneel on the hard cement floor while Poppie delivers endless prayers in Dutch. I don't understand any of it. I can't even speak Afrikaans, let alone Dutch. I sigh and fidget, wanting to be anywhere but where I am. The maid and her daughter, Maisie, attend these prayers, too. Maisie and I peek at each other from between our fingers, trying not to giggle.

I don't remember the train trip home, but these are the fragments of that trip that stand out for me. I have no idea what becomes of the farm after Poppie's death. He has other children, so no doubt it has gone to one of the sons, disregarding Ouma, the eldest child, who almost gave her life for the farm. Patriarchy is alive and well.

Tea, Scones, and Malaria

CHAPTER 7

CANNIBALS AND PUFFADDERS

1954

In 1954 the United States tests its first hydrogen bomb on Bikini Atoll in the Pacific, and Bill Haley and the Comets release "Rock Around the Clock." In the bush, we remain untouched by world events. By the time I am four, we have already lived in three places as we follow Dad around from job to job. No sooner does Mom get comfortable in a home, she must pack up and move again. After leaving the "coronation cake place," we relocate to "the cannibal place" near the Botswana border. At this time, Botswana is known as Bechuanaland, a British protectorate. It is a sparsely populated area, but we have a brick house to live in again for the few months we are there. It is only Mom who is convinced cannibals lurk nearby.

The rumor begins after WW2 when two pilots go missing in this area. The story is they were eaten by cannibals because some local people had been seen wearing their clothes. Where this rumor begins is undetermined. My research shows there is no basis in fact to presume Africans are any more cannibalistic than anyone else, or that this rumor was true. I have since discovered that the real cannibalization of Africa occurred by European occupation, chopping up the continent and its tribes into easily consumable pieces. But white people were conditioned to believe the worst. It all contributed to the incendiary politics and war of later years. False stories don't take much to grow legs.

The rumor persists, and Mom believes it.

"They stand outside and stare," she says to Dad one day at the dinner table. "They're sizing us up for the pot!"

Dad continues to chew. "No cannibals here," he mutters, not even looking up from his plate.

"Then why do they stare at us? Why would anyone *do* that?"

"They don't see a lot of *makiwa* [white people]. They think we're like zoo animals."

"I want to be a lion!" I shout, waving my spoon.

"Shut up and eat!" Mom gives me one of her looks. Small worry lines form around Mom's tight mouth. "What if one of the kids..." She doesn't finish her thought, and Dad only snorts. The people gathering in small groups in front of our house don't bother me one bit. I go over to say hello to them, and they're friendly. The children touch my hair, my face, then pull back as if my hair and skin burn their hands. They giggle. They stare. I stare back. They're pretty strange to me, too. I have had nannies, and we have African servants, but African children are new to me. Except for Poppie's maid's child, I am more used to playing with white kids, but there are no white kids near us.

The savannah here is every bit as dry and desiccated as Bulawayo's, and the infrastructure primitive. The snake population considers the house as much their home as it is ours and slither inside regularly. Puffadders are as plentiful as the groups of people outside staring at us.

During our brief sojourn here, the days are mild and the nights are cold. One evening, Mom walks into the kitchen in her bare feet. Hearing a hiss, she glances down. A sleepy puffadder is curled up near the stove. It pulls itself back into a strike position while Mom's foot, poised to step onto the spot where it lies, freezes in mid-air. Mom's screams are legendary. Her scream of "*Snake!*" can be heard as far away as Bulawayo. Dad drops everything and comes running, brandishing the special snake stick he always keeps nearby; a long, sturdy pole with a fork on one end. He calmly pins the head down while he picks it up behind the head with his bare hands, stuffing the outraged, writhing serpent into a sack that he keeps with the stick.

"I don't kill a snake unless I must," he informs Mom, who, holding onto the door frame, is still trembling from shock. "They really need puffadders at the snake park. I'll take it there tomorrow." And he does. The snake park milks snakes for their venom to make anti-venom.

This is one of the times when I once again vanish. My brother, Rabbit, is a baby, and Mom, as always, busies herself with things that do not involve me. Dad is at the job site. I don't remember this day, but my parents never forget it. After noticing I am missing, Mom doesn't panic right away. She finishes her morning cup of tea, then, with the servants, begins a search of the house and grounds.

After an hour or so, with no sign of me, Dad is summoned from the job. He brings trackers with him—sharp-eyed and keen-eared Africans who can track the spoor of any animal or human. They spend the rest of the day looking for my tracks and conclude I am either a figment of my parent's imagination or I am still in the house.

Mom then does what any other mother would do; she retreats into the living room, sinks into an armchair, and cries. When crying doesn't produce any significant results, she then kneels on the floor, preparing to pray harder than she ever has in her whole life. Mom is quite a faithful supplicant thanks to her religious upbringing. After praying for some time, a strange sound, a scratchy whimper, comes from behind the couch where it sits diagonally across one corner of the living room. She rises from her knees and looks behind the sofa to see the supposedly kidnapped child gazing up at her from the floor with large, terrified eyes.

I have been crouched behind the sofa all day long, making no sound at all. Everyone remembers searching this part of the house repeatedly during the day. I don't know if they looked behind the sofa. I really do not remember this event or why I am there, why no one has heard me, or how a four-year-old can stay, silent, behind a sofa for most of the day. It remains a family mystery, but I have since concluded I must have slept through the commotion.

CHAPTER 8

ZAKA, AN ELEPHANT, AND SILAS

Costume party, Zaka (Pie, age 5, left background)

1955

The "cannibal place" is only a short interlude in our lives. Dad finishes jobs quickly. The government has no trouble finding him another project in another out of the way location. Our lives now have a pattern that contributes to my sense of rootlessness. Yet, at the same time, it also makes me more flexible, something I become accustomed to, and that serves me well in later years. Our next move is more to everyone's liking.

49

We move to a hamlet called Zaka, about fifty miles southeast of Fort Victoria. Dad is to build a bridge here. The small town, with its single main street, consists of about two dozen white families, a few policemen, and a magistrate. I begin my first year of school here, even though I have only just turned five. Mom is my teacher since we have no access to day schools in this area.

Our house is minuscule, but it does have running water and electricity. I remember this year as idyllic, one of the best years of my life. There are children my age I can play with. Life is typical of this era: a family Eden of Norman Rockwell proportions. Mom loves it here, too. We have access to a club with a library, swimming pool, and tennis courts, and plenty of opportunities to socialize with others. The main product of Zaka is gossip and parties. There is no shortage of people to gossip about. With the many parties and social events, loneliness is unknown to anyone in this town.

When someone throws a party, the adults pile their bathed and fed pajama-clad children into the car and set off for the hosts' home. They park the vehicles, leaving us kids in the car while they carouse. Of course, we are meant to be asleep, but we have our own party, talking and laughing from the car windows. We look forward to these parties as much as the adults.

Sometimes there are parties for children, such as the costume party that is hosted by one of the mothers. My memories of this party are vivid because I loathe my costume. I am to be the Queen of Hearts from *Alice in Wonderland*. My dress is made from red crepe paper with hearts pasted all over, and I wear a crown cut from thick craft paper that has been painted gold. It's hideous. Instead, I want to be a fairy. Butch is going as a fairy. She always gets the best things, while I am stuck with being a homely-looking red queen, who, from what I've learned, tries to kill Alice in Wonderland. I want to wear Butch's glittery little tutu made from stiff chiffon, and her gauzy cheesecloth wings. It's not fair! But I go, pouting, to the party and have the best time of my life. I am so energetic from the sugar high from the cakes and soft drinks, I run and run and run around the house and yard, never tiring, then do somersaults over a low hanging tree limb. By the time we get home, my dress is dangling off me in shreds, my hair is matted with something unidentifiable, and I've lost my crown. Butch still looks beautiful with her tutu, wings, and perfectly curled blonde hair.

There is no shortage of servants in these parts, enabling makiwas to enjoy a relaxed social life with frequent parties and get-togethers. Nearly every white person in Rhodesia has servants. It is nothing special, and there probably isn't a white child in southern Africa who has not been raised by an African nanny at some point. We get used to this arrangement: an endless parade of nannies, cooks, houseboys, and gardeners. I like to think the Africans benefit from this arrangement as much as us, but now I suspect they got the short end of the stick. For most Africans, working for white folks is their only opportunity for a job.

In Zaka, we have a cook who I will call "Edward." Edward lives a few hours away via bicycle transport and returns to his home for the weekends. One Monday, Edward is a no-show. That evening, he staggers into the house, face ashen, eyes wide.

"*Au!* Madam," he pants, "the *nzou*...it has destroyed my bike, and nearly killed me! I have walked all the way from Mashoko!"

As he began his return journey over the sandy track that led out of his village, he had been waylaid by a lone bull elephant. It stood in the center of the road, turned to face him, then loudly trumpeted. Edward ditched his bicycle and fled into the surrounding scrub. As he watched, the bull ripped branches and foliage from nearby trees, covering his bike completely. As if that wasn't enough, he leisurely lifted his front leg, bringing his heavy foot down on the bicycle with a sickening crunch.

Edward tried retrieving what was left of his bicycle as soon as the elephant disappeared back into the forest. The elephant had anticipated this. He lurked nearby, and as soon as Edward stepped out onto the road, he bellowed and fake-charged our cook.

Edward discovered that if he ran a short distance away, the elephant would ignore him. His beef seemed to be with the bicycle. Every time Edward attempted to return to the road to retrieve his bike, the elephant charged, and the cook would retreat. Each time, the elephant resumed ripping off branches and foliage, covering the bicycle anew and stomping on it again. Realizing his bike was lost forever, the traumatized man returned on foot, taking nearly all day. Shortly after that, Edward quit. No job was worth defying an enraged elephant.

This is where Silas enters our lives.

Silas has worked with Dad on his construction jobs as a cook for many years. They have developed a firm friendship, as much as possible in the Fifties in Rhodesia, and yet their relationship is still very much employer/employee. But, even at my young age, I know there is a bond between them that transcends race and station.

Silas defects from the construction business to become our cook. He is particularly fond of my brother, Rabbit. Silas does not care much for us girls; we are of no consequence to him, barely rating a two on his importance scale. But Rabbit is another story altogether. Silas fusses over him like an Italian mother.

One day, we are all in trouble with Dad, who is the family disciplinarian. Mom is too soft, according to him, and rarely punishes us for anything. I do not remember if Dad's wrath is over the ripped eider-down comforter and subsequent feather fight business or the uprooted seedling matter in the garden. We know when Dad comes home from work, he means business that will often be expressed at the end of his belt. In today's terms, Dad would be considered abusive. Still, in the Fifties, he is a good and loving father who brooks no nonsense from his offspring. It is how he had been brought up by his strict foster parents, and Dr. Spock be damned. He thinks corporal punishment is the right thing to do. His motto is to "spare the rod and spoil the child." His "rod" is a thick, leather belt. So, we do what many kids would do under the same circumstances. We run away.

We don't run far, but I know how to vanish, as my previous experiences have shown. We flee to the small granite hill—a kopje—not far behind the house and sit under a tree on its far side for a while until we get hungry. Then we wander over to the Dutch lady's home nearby, knowing she will feed us. She always does and treats us as if we are family.

This is where Silas finds us. Dad has sent him out on a reconnaissance mission to find us and bring us home, but Silas cannot bear to see Rabbit punished. He slings Rabbit like a gunny sack over his broad shoulder and disappears with him for the rest of the day, leaving us two girls to face the music alone. I think the Dutch lady intercedes on our behalf. Still, I can't be sure, because we never get the thrashing we expect. Dad never says anything to Silas about the rescue. Africans do not believe in beating children for any reason, at least, not when I lived there.

CHAPTER 9

TURPENTINE

Mom and Dad enjoy painting in oils from our small porch in Zaka. It is one of the only things these two people have in common, other than reading books and writing. In front of the house, a large kopje rises, a mottled gray whaleback from a sea of pink-blooming, red-top savannah grass. This grass blooms at a particular time of the year, so it must be the summer. The feathery foreground grass contrasts with the chunky elephantine boulders that have captured their attention. They are engrossed in precisely portraying how the light falls on these disparate elements.

It is a hot day, and I am thirsty. We must boil all our water before drinking it, so I inform Mom of my thirst. She clicks her tongue as she frowns at her painting. "Will you wait a moment, please?" She sighs and dips her brush into yet another hue. "My grass looks like pink vomit," she informs no one in particular. Dad mutters a distracted "Hmm..." and continues to apply paint to his canvas. I decide I can get water myself. It is kept in the fridge, and I am quite capable of opening the fridge and reaching inside it for the bottled water.

No one is in the kitchen. It is Silas's day off, but standing on the table is what looks like one of our water containers — a repurposed glass bottle that has once contained juice. Filled with a colorless liquid, I assume it is water. The bottle has a label on it, but my reading is rudimentary at best. I have only just started school. I pick up the bottle and take a long swig.

I drop to my knees, my hands clasped around my throat. My chest feels like it is being squeezed in a vice, and my throat burns like hot coals. I can't get my breath. I am trying to cry out for help, but what emerges is a strangled quack. I must pass out almost immediately because I remember nothing until I open my eyes again to an upside-down world. With one hand, Dad holds my convulsing body by the feet, banging me on my back with the other, while Mom pushes a finger down my throat. The purpose of this is to force me to throw up the offending substance or to open up my severely constricted airways. They then spin me upright, pinch my nose shut, and try to force milk down my closed-up throat. Since not even air can get through, the milk dribbles onto the floor.

"She's turning blue!" Mom screams.

"Pound her on the back again!" yells Dad, as he now tries to do whatever other useless *Keystone Kop* thing they have read about somewhere.

Mom pounds me. I choke even more, but finally, I manage to get out an ear-piercing howl, which turns into a deep, wheezing gulp of air that rushes into my starved lungs. For the next few minutes, all I can do is pant, heave, and choke. Finally, my face turns its typical shade of pink, and I breathe easier, but my throat hurts for a long time after. It is only later that I realize I have swallowed turpentine. The bottle is meant for oil paintbrush cleaning, and the label states "Turpentine" very clearly, only I cannot yet read that word.

There are no hospitals, clinics, or doctors nearby. If you get sick, you make the long trek over rough roads to Fort Victoria. Somehow, I survive the turpentine incident. Apparently, it does not cause any long-term effects.

I am five years old and can already read some words (but not "turpentine"). I go into the pantry where Mom stores her canned goods and read the labels on the cans. In the bush, there are no schools nearby. White people at this time do not attend African schools and vice versa. How much easier it would be on my family if we are able to mix with the larger child population in the native reserves. Not only is the language a barrier for us in the Fifties, it's an unheard-of option for white kids, and similarly for black kids. We cannot attend each other's schools.

The whites, the makiwa, send their offspring to boarding schools in the larger cities or they are home-schooled. I am now a pupil of "School on the Air." We own a sizeable two-way shortwave radio that runs on batteries. Every morning we connect with the government-run classes in Salisbury. I begin my first year of Kindergarten here, and then it is time to move, again.

Both this town and the cannibal place are important stopping-off places in our lives, like wayside inns, where we can rest before the long trek through real hardship country begins. Things are due for a change. Dad has completed the bridge in this area and has been assigned another bridge. This one is in the Lowveld.

Tea, Scones, and Malaria

CHAPTER 10

NUANETSI AND PETINA

1957

Ghana has already gained its independence from Great Britain, but in Rhodesia, we remain a dominion, a British colony. Dad's job as a builder takes us to increasingly under-developed areas to create an infrastructure, and this year, we become Lowveld pioneers.

In the south-eastern quadrant of Rhodesia, the Lowveld consists mainly of Tribal Trust areas, or what is known as "Native Reserves." This vast area is as empty of infrastructure and towns as the Namib Desert. There are no developed areas or other white people here, except for a sprinkling of Christian missionaries. A bridge needs to be built over the Nuanetsi [now the Mwenezi] River. The area where we are to live is called Buffalo Bend.

We pack our bags and animals—a young black cat named, you guessed it, Blackie and our Wiener dog, Fritz— into the Land Rover and set off for the Lowveld, so named for being a low-lying basin in the south-eastern part of the country. The lushness of Zaka surrenders to an arid scrubland of ochre soil and brown grass dotted with mopane trees. The air is hot and humid. Mom fans herself with a magazine. She bites her lip as the road dwindles to a mere track, and the Land Rover jounces from pothole to rut to crater, making us long for the dirt roads of Zaka.

Like my siblings, I consider it all an enormous adventure as the Land Rover, piled high with family possessions, at long last pulls up to our future home. The sky is darkening to the east as the sun sinks in an orange ball behind the spreading cordyla, or sunbird trees, which line the nearby riverbank. Dusk arrives quickly in the tropics. Our yowling cat, Blackie, is as overjoyed to arrive as we are. He shoots out of the Land Rover like a dark arrow and heads off into the mopane scrub, acacia, and black-fruited nyala trees behind our new abode. This environment suits the mostly feral Blackie to the core. Fritz, our Wiener dog, is less adventurous. His big brown eyes survey the alien landscape from the vehicle as if it will swallow him whole. We toss him out.

To say our house is a dump is an understatement. What we see is not a brick home with a tin roof. It is not even a home. It does fit the description of a shack, though. Made entirely of corrugated tin, the shanty sits on a cement slab, a smaller tin construction, Dad's workshop, squatting next to it. This, Dad proudly informs us, is our new home.

Noticing Mom's crestfallen expression and fixed smile, Dad is quick to explain the larger shanty will be only a temporary shelter. Mom always tries to appear cheerful and optimistic in front of her children, even if it kills her. The three-hour drive over dusty tracks that pass for roads in this part of the country has left everyone exhausted and dirty. The humidity and high heat do nothing to raise our spirits.

"All I want is a hot bath and a comfortable bed," Mom sighs as she stretches and gets out of the Land Rover. Dad doesn't say anything but gives her nervous glances as he begins to unload our luggage.

I step out of the Land Rover and dig my dirty bare feet into the red-tinged, welcoming soil. Fritz, having recovered his aplomb, signifies his approval by anointing the area with leg lifts. Everyone except Mom seems excited and happy to be here. I sniff the heavy scented, humid air that smells like freshly baked bread. The flowers of the potato bush shrub produce a distinct aroma of baked potatoes in the early evening. Still, to me, it smells more like bread baking. A cacophony of sounds meets my ears. The stentorian *go-away!* of the gray loerie, the *ask-father* cry of a turtle dove, the joyful notes of the black-headed bulbuls, a chirruping of glossy starlings, a chorus of frogs in a nearby river pool, and not least, the sonorous croak of a bullfrog.

Dad explains he has placed the shack close to the river so that we don't have far to go for water. The river water is pumped into forty-four-gallon drums located near our shack. He leads us inside, the faint, worried look still hovering on his face. The corrugated tin walls sit on a cement floor. A flat tin roof overhead makes the inside of the shack feel like an oven, its windows propped open with wooden two-by-fours to let in a non-existent breeze. The interior walls separate bedrooms, a bathroom, and a living room. The kitchen, a lean-to huddled next to the shack, consists of a wood-burning stove, a table, and a paraffin freezer. Paraffin, or "kerosene," freezers are used in areas without electric power. [Kerosene fuels a burner which allows the ammonia in the freezer to evaporate and cool. I failed science, but this is how I understand the technical parts.] Our meager furniture—chairs, tables, and beds—has already been arranged in some semblance of familiarity. In the bathroom, a tin tub sits on the concrete floor, a brown ring still adhering to the interior hinting at the water's color in which we'll be luxuriating. Mom's smile vanishes for a brief second but reappears when Dad reminds us that he has begun building a new house, a real home, on the banks of the river further upstream.

We are delighted with his descriptions of our new abode. It will be one that sits on a hill and possesses a panoramic view of the pools where the big game come to drink. We are not able to see the river from the shack site. Our view is blocked by thick scrub and trees.

Silas emerges from his quarters nearby, welcoming us with a happy smile and a hissing Tilly lamp. Silas can adjust to hardship easier than these soft white people. Little do these particular white people know that this place is only the beginning of an extraordinary and memorable life.

I wonder what Silas must think about the fragile makiwas in his environment. Sure, he knows Dad is a pro and can easily survive this lifestyle, but he must wonder about the *maðam*, as white women are referred to, and the three children. Silas is a Ndebele, an offshoot of the Zulu tribe that settled in what is now Rhodesia in the 1800s. The local Africans in this south-eastern part of the country are of the Mashona (Shona or Rozwi) tribe. At this time, the Shona live close to the land and have no use for the white man's modern ways or conveniences. However, they are practical, and this is where Petina enters our lives.

Not long after our arrival, Mom begins to find it increasingly difficult to cope with the bush's hardships and three small children. She can't expect Silas to do it all. Word spreads by bush telegraph that the white madam is looking for a nanny. She has one applicant—Petina. Petina has attended a Tribal Trust school for a few years, where she learned to speak some English. Mom and us children speak a smattering of *Fanegalo*, a pigeon-mix of Shona and English, so in this way, we communicate with Petina. Rabbit, thanks to our previous nanny, Violetta, speaks nothing but Chikaranga, another local tribal lingo. He still has trouble speaking English, but he is learning.

It is possible that Petina probably has an even more difficult time communicating with Silas than she does with her white employers. The Shona and Ndebele languages are vastly different and have always presented a problem in their political history. It is almost like having Italians and Germans living together under one roof, and neither has learned the other's language. Yet, they are expected to get along and understand each other at the same time because they're both European. This is the case in Africa with its numerous fragmented tribes and languages.

Petina is a raw recruit. A statuesque girl, even for her young age, which is most likely in her late teens, she says she does not know how old she is—not an uncommon thing in Africa. Africans do not celebrate birthdays as white people do. She has applied for the job because she is blind in one eye, most possibly from a childhood injury or disease. She never tells anyone her story. Still, it prevents her from making a good marriage amongst her tribe. Life in the bush community is harsh. It favors the survival of the fittest, and she has a handicap. Still, Mom does not find it a problem, so Petina becomes a part of our family.

African women are wonderful with children, very gentle and loving. Petina is all of these things, but short on patience. She does not tolerate any foolishness from us as we learn over the years. If we transgress, she threatens us with a variety of mythical African monsters, *shaves*, and *ngozis*: shades and avenging spirits of the dead, but most notably, the *tokoroshe*, or *chikwambo*. The tokoroshe is a sprite, a dwarf-like creature that causes mischief in the home or even illness and death. The only person who can banish a tokoroshe is the *nganga*, the witchdoctor or diviner, and Petina considers the nganga an even more fearsome entity.

"*Ai*! You will bring tokoroshe upon us, you bad child! And then, the nganga will come, and…" Her blind eye stares whitely at us as she clucks her tongue, towering over us, brows drawn together as she extricates us from whatever situation we have gotten ourselves into.

Petina never wears shoes, and she always wears a loose-fitting cotton dress with a colorful scarf tied around her head. The soles of her feet are hard and callused, and like Petina, we too roam the bushveld in our bare feet, walking over scorching earth and through patches of thorns as if they are a carpeted floor. Our feet are like Petina's.

Each morning, as soon as we rise, we head off into the bush to play. We don't come home until we are hungry. Every day three children aged seven, five, and four years old are exposed to incredible dangers that children of any age will never be exposed to in any first-world society. Elephants, lions, leopards, snakes, scorpions, and other potentially dangerous animals or critters all roam within spitting distance from the tin shack.

Petina does not solicitously follow us around like most nannies do. She and Mom agree, thanks to Mom's reliance on Dr. Spock, that it is good to let us run around the bush as we please, like African children.

Mom is very laid back. She must be, in this environment. Some may consider Mom neglectful. I see it more as a backlash against her own upbringing with dysfunctional, neurotic parents, and perhaps also a hallmark of the era. Mom shows us in many ways that she loves us and cares about our welfare, but she isn't the helicopter mother like Ouma had been for her. Mom treats her children as little adults and never over-reacts to the dangers we face from the bush. In retrospect, I think she wanted us to learn how to function on our own, to grow up to be independent and self-reliant.

The river meanders wide with sandy banks and large pools where elephant and other game come to drink. Our favorite place to play is in the sandy bed of the river. It is our sandbox. The footprints the elephants make are so big we can sit in them. Water seeps up from the riverbed, filling the indentations, and we each have our own small pool. We have been told never to go into the larger pools of water because of the crocodiles, and we have been shown areas where it is safe to swim and where it is not. If the water is shallow and fast flowing, we can safely play in these areas, but not the deeper pools.

The other danger in our lives from the water is the parasitic disease *bilharzia*. One day, I overhear Mom and Dad discussing this disease since it is a constant and frequent threat.

"Watch out for an itchy, red rash," Dad said. "It means the worm has gotten through your skin.

Mom scratches her arm. "I think I have it. Maybe it's in our bath water."

"That's a mozzie bite. We should all be tested for it, anyway. It will be surprising if none of us get it."

"How would we know if we had it? Can you die from it?" Mom's quick, frightened glance at me lurking nearby tells me that this *bill* thing isn't anything I want to get.

"Maybe eventually it can kill you if you don't get treatment," Dad goes on to say, ignoring the eavesdropper. "Gives you a fever. The worm gets into your body through the skin. If you see snails in stagnant, green water, it means bilharzia is there too. The snails are the host."

"I'm taking the kids in to see the doctor next time we're in Fort Vic. They're always in the water."

Dad shrugs, but the look on his face tells me he's concerned.

I leave, feeling unsettled. I swim in the river every day. I even drink the river water when no one is looking, but I feel fine. I run outside, forgetting the conversation almost immediately. We are going to swim in the river this afternoon. I haven't noticed any snails in the area where we swim. I wade in the clear water that bubbles over white stones and try to scoop up the tiny fish that dart between our fingers. Today we will look for frog's eggs—foamy globs on the bank that remind me of cotton candy (*candy floss*, as we call it) but doesn't taste anything like candy floss. This *bill* thing just isn't worth worrying about.

We take long hikes through the bush, alone and barefoot. We carry sticks and think we're invincible. Not once do we ever catch sight of an animal, even in this wildlife paradise, but we know they are there. Not once has anything ever attacked us. We feel as safe in this environment as in our home, and in a way, it is our home. We have become as much a part of the bush as its animals and flora. Maybe we are just lucky, or perhaps we are not seen as threat or prey, but it never occurs to us to feel threatened at any time.

There are some exceptions, though, such as the day we take a family hike through the bush. Walking in single file along a path, a track made by animals, Dad is in front, Mom behind him. The rest of us follow. When things happen in the bush, they happen fast. Dad is the first to spot the cobra rearing up on the path ahead, its yellowish, hooded head swaying back and forth.

"Back!" Dad shouts, freezing in place. Our eyes wide with terror, we hurriedly backpedal to a safer distance, but, like Dad, we don't turn and run. Dad does not have his rifle or even a stick with him. Dad and the cobra make eye contact, and face to face, they stare at each other for what feels like a lifetime. The cobra head weaves slightly, forked tongue flicking in and out in this game of Statues. It seems to be as tall as Dad, its tail still hidden in the long grass on either side of the path. We don't dare speak. Another eon passes, and finally, the cobra slowly lowers its body, coiling itself back into the grass and slithering away, back into the dry grass from which it emerged. We all relax but wait another eternity until we are sure it isn't still lurking nearby. With a sigh of relief, we turn and make our way home.

CHAPTER 11

BUSH CUISINE

In a tin shack with no circulating air or electricity, the heat in the first months we are here is oppressive. We stay outdoors as much as possible during the day, playing by the river near the cool shady pools. We only come back in the late afternoon for our supper, cooked by Silas on a wood stove in the outdoor kitchen. Our evening meal is always the main meal of the day. Dad frequently hunts for impala and kudu meat that supplies his workforce with food. We rarely eat beef, chicken, or pork. On the menu is either the venison Dad brings home or the bream that Dad and I catch in the river with a hand line.

Dad often takes me fishing. Rabbit is still too young to trust with a hook, so Dad takes me down to the river, to the deep, rocky pools where river bream, catfish, and barbel are plentiful. He teaches me how to place a worm on the end of my hook and then helps me throw the line into the deepest part of the pool. Dad encourages me not to talk.

"It scares the fish away," he says, so we just sit for hours, each lost in our thoughts. The sun sparkling on the surface of the water makes my eyes droop. On a nearby branch, a giant kingfisher ruffles its feathers, shaking its shaggy crest. Its *kee-kee-ou* call draws my attention away from the water.

"You have a bite!" Dad yells, shaking me out of my trance.

I jump as the line slides through my slack fingers. Something is pulling it out of my hand. I grip the line as tightly as I can, and Dad runs to my side, adding his strength to my feeble grasp. Finally, the line tautens, and we begin to pull, Dad yelling encouragement as I squeal in delight. I have finally caught a fish.

"It's a big one!" Dad whoops, his face red with excitement. "Pull harder!" He doesn't want to take any credit for this one, so he moves behind me to ensure I do not drop the line. I pull and pull, puffing with effort, my fingers burning from the strain. Without warning, something flops out of the water and onto the rock where I am standing. Aghast, I stare at it for a moment as Dad nets the squirming thing and lifts it away from the water's edge.

"It's a barbel!" Dad says, with a catch of pride in his voice. "A big one! Silas will know how to cook it for us."

Whatever it is, I don't like it. I scream and back away from the slimy, elongated fish with its ugly, flat head, a head that sprouts long, spiny barbs around a wide mouth with sharp teeth. To me, it is a monster, a shave risen from the depths of the black lagoon. Dad takes a long look at my face and throws the squirming, flopping fish back.

Later, on another fishing trip at the same fishing hole, I catch a river bream, a favorite eating fish. At least, I think I have caught it and cry all the way home when Dad does not throw this one back. (Many years later, Dad admits to me he placed it on my line when I wasn't looking.) That night, Silas prepares the bream for our dinner, and Dad announces to all that it is "the fish that Pie caught," but try as I might, I can't eat that fish. I am now a murderer.

We dine like the locals, using the cornmeal staple sadza, or alternately, potatoes or rice. Our vegetables are canned. The monthly excursions to Fort Victoria are for what we can store in the small kerosene freezer or in a make-shift pantry. I am constipated nearly all the time from a lack of fiber. My siblings and I suffer constant worm infections from walking barefoot outside or not washing our hands properly. Digestive problems plague us all. Like a clutch of kittens, we must be dewormed regularly by drinking a foul concoction Mom has purchased from the pharmacy in Fort Victoria. It is called "Rid," a hideous pink syrup with a chemical, sweet flavor that makes us gag.

Petina teaches us to catch and eat what she eats: fat mopane worms that are not worms but pale caterpillars that feed on the mopane tree leaf. She prepares these for us by squeezing their innards out and hanging them out to dry. We crunch down on the salty snack as if they are pretzels. Petina eats them cooked in a stew, but this is where Mom draws the line at bush food. We also snack on flying ants — termites — at the beginning of the rainy season when they swarm in search of new colonies, frying them golden brown in butter. Petina constructs a grass tunnel around the largest hole on an anthill with a small basin of water at its entrance that catches the winged ants as they emerge. To us children, a snack of termites is as tasty as a Big Mac or pizza is to today's child. Petina also teaches us to gather the fallen gourd-like pods of the baobab tree with its sour, chalky fruit. However, she gravely warns us we are not to overeat the fruit since it makes an effective purging medicine in larger quantities. We ignore this rule regularly, but it solves the problem of constipation very nicely.

Dad's favorite snack, and ours, is *biltong*. Biltong is called jerky in the United States, but it is there where all resemblance ends. Dad cuts strips of lean meat from an antelope, usually kudu or impala, marinating the thin strips in a vinegar solution, salt, and other ingredients. He keeps tweaking the marinade to get just the right combination, and Dad's biltong is still the best I've ever eaten. When he deems the meat has absorbed enough of the liquid, he dries the strips off, rubs them with spices, and hangs each piece on a wire strung across an interior room. He can only make biltong during the dry winter months when the humidity is at its lowest. The drying process usually takes several weeks; it is ready when it has the consistency of old shoe leather. Dad takes a sharp knife and cuts it up for us, but sometimes he slices it thinly using his woodworking plane as one would use a slicing mandolin. Of all the traditional African foods, this one is our favorite.

We love the winter months when biltong is our staple, when the nights are cool, when the mosquitoes are whittled down to a manageable minimum, and when we can easily spot wildlife through the bare, brown trees. Winter, or what passes for it in this part of the world, always seems to end abruptly. It catapults us into the rainy season like a stone out of a slingshot. We are about to experience an unforgettable display of the ferocity of an African storm.

CHAPTER 12

THE STORM

I am six years old. It is a sultry night in November 1956 when our rainy season arrives. It sweeps in on a gale-force wind — a raging armada, cloud sails billowing in a dark and moonless sky.

Blackie has come indoors, which should be our first clue something is going to happen. Along with Fritz, he climbs on the bed and does not move, not even when the howling wind lifts the shack from its cement foundation, first one corner and then another. As each blast lifts an edge, snakes, spiders, and scorpions scuttle or slide in, seeking shelter from the raging elements. Mom and Dad witness this invasion in every flash of lightning that lights up the night like a fireworks display. The pelting rain sounds like machine-gun fire hitting the tin roof.

"I want to check on the kids," Mom says, her voice muffled because the blanket is pulled over her head. Dad snorts.

"They'll be fine if they don't get out of bed. Stay here, you don't know what's on the floor."

"But the shack's going to blow away!"

"It won't. It's too heavy. It's only the sides that are lifting up. I'll anchor it better in the morning..." His voice trails off as another clap of thunder crashes overhead.

73

Finally, concern for her children's safety overcomes Mom's terror of what may be lurking on the floor. She bounds off the bed during a lull, slipping her feet into her shoes. The first indication something is amiss is a shrill scream that makes Dad's blood run cold. Without thinking, Dad leaps off the bed, not pausing to put on his shoes, running barefoot to Mom's rescue. Dueling shrieks now echo through the tin shack. Dad has stepped on a scorpion, while Mom's foot has encountered one of these critters hiding out in her shoe. Scorpions do not take this sort of treatment lightly. They sting first and ask questions later.

Mom and Dad dance around in agony, each clutching a foot that will swell to twice its size in days to come, in the worst pain that either of them can imagine.

We children do not hear the commotion from our parents over the bedlam of the storm. Butch and I have been making bets that the shack will blow away and end up in the river. I reach out to Blackie, who is crouching on my bed, yellow eyes glowing like lamps. He hisses, and I pull my hand back. He has not been well-socialized. Fritz is under the blanket on Butch's bed. I can see the blanket quivering as he shivers and shakes with each thunder clap. Rabbit is kneeling on his bed in a prayerful position. Butch points at him, butt in the air, face resting on his pillow.

"He's asleep, isn't he?"

I nod, giggling. "He falls asleep like that all the time!"

In the morning, we carefully shake out our shoes, but since we don't wear shoes anyway, it is an exercise in futility. The concrete floor of the shack is streaked with sandy soil and debris. Critters scurry into dark corners. Mom shrieks. Silas takes it all in his stride, bringing out a straw broom to vigorously sweep away all evidence of the night's activity. We run outside to take a look at the aftermath of the storm. Other than some branches down, everything looks much the same as before, except muddier.

Mom and Dad hobble around on painful feet for days afterward, but again we are lucky. This particular variety of scorpion, small and black with a fiery sting, is not one of those that can kill an elephant.

Dad forgets his promise to secure the tin shack. Mom and Dad's feet are swollen with red and purple patches. Africa teaches us that it is essential to give our shoes a thorough shake before putting them on. They are ideal hiding places for scorpions and other unpleasant creatures.

We live in the tin shack for no more than a few months. Dad doesn't play. In between his work on the bridge, he has completed our house at Buffalo Bend.

Tea, Scones, and Malaria

CHAPTER 13

BUFFALO BEND

1957

At last, the house that is to become our permanent home is complete. 'Permanence' to our family now means we will be in a place perhaps a year or two but not much longer than that. Once the bridge is built, we will move on to the next project. The house is magnificent. Anything after the tin shack is an improvement, but this house is more suited to the climate than the shack. It also feels like home. It sits in a small clearing, overlooking a sweeping bend in the river known as Buffalo Bend.

Dad has built the house in typical African style, an adobe brick bungalow, its high walls whitewashed to a gleaming white. The roof is a thick thatch of durable savannah grass with high beamed ceilings that keep us dry and the air cool and circulating. The whole house feels fresh and inviting, and even in this hot climate there is no need for air-conditioners. It is only many years later that we acquire the luxury of air conditioning. Without electricity, it is not an option. Wet washcloths draped over foreheads become our inadequate, low-tech solution on the hottest nights.

A verandah, enclosed with wire-mesh gauze to keep the insects out, runs the length of the house. We sit here in the late afternoon and early evening, drinking tea and watching the animals that gather at the shaded, deep pool in the bend of the river. Zebra, giraffe, buffalo, wildebeest, impala, kudu, and other antelope, along with the "Big Five"—lions, elephants, rhino, leopard, and buffalo—abound. Screeching monkeys, baboons, warthogs, and water birds of all kinds regularly show up.

Many years later, I find a note written by Mom she has inserted into a book about the area, now a rest camp at Buffalo Bend:

"When we left in 1959 only our house (the present rest camp) stood there and the bridge which Dad built. We used to watch the elephants and other game drinking and sporting in the waterhole from our verandah."

On clear nights, the Milky Way overhead provides a backdrop for the scene below. We do some stargazing with Dad's theodolite, the fancy name for a surveyor's telescope. Dad teaches us the names and locations of constellations and planets. We gaze at the moon through the telescope and are amazed at how close it seems: as if we could reach out and touch it.

A few feet away from the house stands a magnificent baobab tree, its gnarled branches reaching for the sky. The wrinkled, grey-barked, bulbous, and pithy baobab tree with its colossal girth looks like a giant redwood that has been uprooted and buried upside down. The trees are short and squat; the trunks' circumferences varying from less than ten feet to over a hundred feet. Our tree is approximately thirty feet in circumference.

It does not take us long to discover that we have built our home on an elephant walk. Enormous gray ghosts silently move around the house at night, seeking the original path they carved out so many years ago. The baobab tree is a vital way station, a rest stop, for the elephants who like to eat its bark. Lions, too, enjoy the tree. They bring what they kill elsewhere to eat here, under the baobab, as if it is their favorite wildlife restaurant. We are lulled to sleep nightly by the growls and roars that soon become part of the background bush orchestra.

Another tree grows closer to the house, a massive tree that provides beautiful shade. During another storm, it uproots and topples, its main trunk and canopy missing the house by mere feet. We are lucky not to be squashed like *mozzies*.

The bush teaches us that all bathroom business must be conducted during daylight hours. There is no getting up at night to wander down the small path that leads to the grass and pole outhouse behind the house. Health reasons places the toilet some distance from the home, and a bucket filled with lime stands nearby so we can toss a few cupfuls down the pit to keep the odor down. During daylight hours, one can safely enter, but with caution. Snakes or other unsavory creatures might find shelter here. But at night, unless it is a dire emergency, visits to the outhouse are discouraged. We have long ago learned how to make use of the chamber pot. Each bedroom contains at least one, and if one must use it, it is emptied in the morning.

One night, Mom suffers a bout of diarrhea. Not wanting to use the chamber pot, she grabs the paraffin Tilley lamp, pumping it up until the wick is glowing with the most energetic light it can muster. Making her way cautiously down the path to the outhouse, she glances nervously over her shoulder toward the baobab. Luckily, the regulars are not hanging out there this night, but her luck does not last. In her desperate state, she forgets to check the outhouse before entering. The sense of urgency makes her more careless than usual.

Placing the lamp on the floor, she settles down onto the wide, wooden seat. It is only then that she glances up, gazing into a slit-eyed, fanged, and equally startled face. A snake of unknown lineage has curled itself around one of the poles only inches away. Mom does not take the time, as Dad would have done, to discover whether or not it comes from one of the more toxic families inhabiting these parts. Her shrieks interrupt the bush night orchestra as she breaks all Olympic records getting back to the house, panties still at half-mast. Later, Mom swears to us she has found the cure for diarrhea since she did not have any problem with it for the rest of the night.

Bathroom facilities are only slightly better than those of the shack. The galvanized iron tin tub has come with us. We now also have a "donkey boiler," a forty-four-gallon drum of rain or river water that is heated over a brick fireplace next to the house.

Since we kids are outdoors most of the day when I am not being home-schooled, we arrive back at the house around dusk, covered in dirt, looking like clay golems. Petina *tch-tch's*, placing us in the tub, soaping us from head to toe, and scrubbing us with a rough loofah as if we are greasy kitchen pots. We cry out in pathetic voices, but Petina persists until we emerge like cooked lobsters from the tub, all red and shiny.

Our drinking water in the bush must be boiled and stored in our kerosene-run fridge. In the indoor kitchen. Oh, what luxury! We fill our pantry with canned and dry goods. Mom bakes regularly, and we now eat scones with our tea. Mom is a poor cook, but she has discovered it is almost impossible to ruin a scone. We eat them with butter and jam. Cream is still an unheard-of luxury for us.

We keep chickens in the back yard, inside an enclosure. We have eggs aplenty, and the occasional chicken is dispatched by Silas for a Sunday dinner. Dad keeps an incubator on the verandah to hatch chickens from some of the eggs. We always have fluffy little yellow chicks to replenish our egg-layers and broilers.

While we do not miss the trappings of civilization, it is helpful for Mom to have something to eat besides kudu or impala meat. She is becoming accustomed to the solitariness of bush-life, and even the lack of a social life. I think she enjoys the peace and quiet and gets lost in a book or in one of her paintings. I hear the typewriter clacking away many days as she writes her poetry and short stories.

"Go outside and play," she'll tell us, waving her hand, a distracted look on her face. "Can't you see I'm busy?" We don't need much encouragement. The screen door slams, and we're gone until nearly sunset when Petina is sent out to scout for her missing charges, placing us, protesting, in the tin tub, and the torturous scrub-down begins.

Tea, Scones, and Malaria

Dad doesn't really miss his makiwa friends. He is a natural for the bush—an introvert who enjoys his own company—but he does find fellowship in Silas, who is much like Dad. They possess the same sense of humor. It is only a matter of time before they put their heads together and come up with some buffoonery, ways to amuse themselves at the expense of Dad's workers.

CHAPTER 14

KARMA NEVER SLEEPS

I t isn't easy finding workers for the bridge. Dad has a handful of skilled workers, but city Africans do not want to go into the bush to work. Most of his workers were born in the city and have never left it before coming here. They are nervous in this environment. The local Africans are not trained in this sort of work, so it is nearly impossible to hire anyone locally. It gets so bad that the government begins to import workers from cities in South Africa — Johannesburg in particular. His crew consists of workers from the gold mines in the area called the Rand — Dad's old training ground where he received his Builder's Certificate.

It's difficult to know what promises have lured these workers to the bundu but they come and go quickly. The first lorry [truck] load of about two dozen men leave in a hurry. An elephant mistook their hut for a baobab tree, using it as a scratching post for its itchy hide. The workers, seeing their shelter moving from side to side, unwisely decided to investigate. Upon opening the hut door, the bravest investigator found himself standing between four pillars of solid elephant flesh.

After the second or third lorry goes hurtling back to the cities, Dad and Silas decide they might have some fun with the next load. They will most likely be leaving anyway. True to their expectations, the next lorry arrives full of wide-eyed, apprehensive townies. Silas tells Dad, scorn dripping from every word, "Ay! They jump at every snapping twig or bush noise. At night, they huddle together in their mud and grass huts like frightened aunties." Dad and Silas begin to concoct their plans.

Not long after they arrive, the new crew are safely tucked away in their hut on a moonless night, eating their meal of sadza and impala meat. Dad, with an old paraffin tin, and Silas, with a sizeable brittle tree branch, slowly creep up to the hut. Dad is familiar with animal noises. He can easily imitate any animal by forcing air through his pursed lips, using his cupped hands. He also uses an empty paraffin can, lending timbre and authority to a roar or shriek. Taking his deepest breath, he blows a long, loud elephant trumpet—a piercing screech—into the can. At the same time, Silas snaps the tree limb over his knee.

Stifling their laughter, they watch as the townies, about a dozen of them, all try to pile into the cab of the lorry at the same time. By the next morning, they, too, are gone.

I don't know how Dad ever solves his labor problem. However, the bridge gets built eventually and still stands over the river to this day.

Not all is a joke, though. Dad has his own unforgettable experience with an elephant that causes him severe psychological trauma and bad dreams for years to come. On one of his excursions to replenish the meat supply, he takes a young African gun bearer who has one job: to carry the rifle. As Dad steps into a clearing, he stops abruptly, his mouth hanging open. An elephant cow and her calf are in the clearing, taking their afternoon siesta. The wind direction favors the elephant. As soon as she catches a whiff of the humans in her vicinity—one carrying a rifle—she lifts her trunk and bellows, her legs pumping clouds of dust. At close quarters, it must sound like a shriek from hell, and with ears flapping like sails and trunk raised, the cow begins to charge.

Dad turns to the gun bearer for his rifle, which fortunately, is capable of shooting elephants. While Dad has never shot an elephant in his life, he is prepared to protect himself and the bearer. He hopes, too, that the rifle shot will scare her off. But there is no bearer. He has fled, taking the rifle with him. There is only one thing left to do; Dad does something he never thinks he will ever do. He turns tail and runs.

Dad is not a runner by any means, but that day he breaks all sprinting records. As he runs, he can hear the crashing and bellowing behind him, drawing closer, closer. It informs some part of his brain that can still function that the elephant is not playing games. She is furious and wants to expunge this disrespectful human from the earth forever. He dares not look back. His legs pumping, he leaps over fallen logs like an Olympic hurdler and careens around rocks, termite mounds, and other obstacles as if he is a ball propelled from a pinball machine plunger. His heart beats so fast he feels he will surely drop dead of a heart attack before the elephant has a chance to trample him or impale him with her tusks. His breath comes out in long, wheezing gasps and his legs begin to falter. The cow is gaining on him. He feels her hot breath on his neck from the waving trunk that reaches out for him.

From deep down, Dad musters every bit of adrenaline he still possesses and increases his pace. The muscles in his legs burn as he pushes them to the limit, his breath whistling as he tries to pull more air into his straining lungs. He begins to wonder how much longer he can keep the pace up.

An eternity seems to pass when, through the scrub, he sees our house's white walls glinting through the trees. Encouraged, he surges forward, breaking through the trees, and lurches, legs shaking, up onto the verandah steps. Fumbling with the screen door latch, he collapses, exhausted, onto the verandah floor in front of his startled wife and daughter, still immersed in School on the Air.

"What...?" Mom asks. She rises and runs to his side, but Dad can't talk. His breath emerges in raw heaves and a face so pale we think he might pass out. A minute or so elapses as he collects himself, calms his breathing, then slowly rises onto wobbly legs and looks outside.

Nothing. A profound silence and an empty yard meet his gaze. It is as if nothing has ever happened, but he knows he has just outrun an elephant, something few people ever live to tell. The enraged cow no doubt broke off the chase as soon as the house came into view. Mom and I hadn't even seen it.

Dad never fully recovers from this experience. For many years after that, he suffers nightmares of being chased by an elephant. Although attacks are uncommon, when an elephant comes across a human that it considers threatening, it will kneel on the human, crushing them. It's rare to survive this.

That day, though, I am relieved Dad did not shoot the elephant. Her calf would not have survived as an orphan.

Every time he goes out on a hunting expedition to shoot meat for his workers and us, I always hope he will come back empty-handed, even if it means we'll forfeit our daily venison, and heaven forbid, our beloved biltong. We are carnivores, as much as the lion or cheetah, yet I still loathe the killing part of it all. When he brings a dead impala or kudu home and strings it up under the baobab tree to skin and gut, I weep.

On one of our return trips from Fort Victoria, with us three kids sitting in the backseat, Dad suddenly hits the brake on the Land Rover, pulls off the road, and reaches for his rifle. He isn't going to miss a serendipitous opportunity to stock up on our meat supply. It is not only us he must feed, but his workers as well. A barely visible impala doe stands motionless in the nearby mopane shade, staring at us with velvety eyes, her large ears twitching. Realizing what Dad intends, we begin to wail and sob in the back seat.

"Don't shoot, Dad!" we beg. "Run!" we scream at the doe, banging our fists and feet on the side of the Land Rover. After staring at us for much too long, the impala, with a toss of her head, bounds into the scrub. Dad scowls, placing his rifle back onto its rack. We continue on, but Dad mutters under his breath all the way home.

"You eat meat, don't you? You don't complain about the biltong, either. Do you think I enjoy this? You like your biltong, don't you? Do you think biltong grows on a bush...do you think that it's easy for me to traipse into the bush once a week and kill something? How would you like to..." and on it goes as we sit, silent but satisfied in the back seat, knowing that at least for one day, we've spared an animal from the cooking pot.

Mom directs an enigmatic smile at us. I think she understands.

CHAPTER 15

CHRISTMAS CICADAS

Octber is known generally as a month when, if you need a reason to kill yourself, it might be at this time of year. October is a blasted, infernal month of relentless heat that seems to stretch into eternity. It is the time between seasons, before the rains arrive, when the dry months of the winter season reluctantly give way to summer. A hush descends over the desiccated, dusty plain. Animals take shelter in the sparse shade, and we humans fan our faces with whatever flat object we can find that moves the air. The temperature soars, and the barren, blanched river beds glare bright under the relentless sun. Not a breeze stirs, and waves of heat shimmer on the dry river bed. Animals search frantically for the water that will slake their thirst. Our pool at the bend has shrunk into a muddy, stagnant smudge on white-hot sand.

It is only in November that the thunderheads build up, towering gray battleships driven by gusty breezes. In the bush, twirling dust devils cavort, while the smell of distant raindrops on chalky soil lends a briskness to the atmosphere. Butch, Rabbit, and I lift our faces, sniffing the rejuvenated air, then the first raindrops fall—whopping splats that hit us in the face as we run outside, bare naked, to feel the onslaught. We scream in delight as the pelting rain hits our skinny, pale asses.

"Get in the house now!" Mom shouts from the verandah. "What do you think you're doing?"

We laugh and squeal, opening our mouths to catch the fat drops. We take deep breaths, inhaling the dusty rain smell as the steaming earth rejoices with us to receive nature's bountiful blessing. A headshaking, *ah-ah-ing* Petina rounds us up, then herds us, like *mombies* [African cattle] indoors, dripping, but satisfied. She shepherds us into the bedroom where we left our clothes.

"Nekkid not good." She makes a clucking sound with her tongue, her lips tight as we put our clothes back on. "Nganga will get you. Use for *muti*!" She mumbles. Muti is African medicine. Children were once a prime source of the evil practice of harvesting body parts, witchcraft magic that may yet be endemic to some rural areas. But threats often work where other things fail. We never run outside naked again.

By December, the rains have turned the brittle veldt into a lush green grassland where food is plentiful, and the river becomes a swollen deluge that sweeps huge chunks of debris downstream. Work on the bridge ceases, and many workers go home for the Christmas holidays.

Instead of sleigh bells and carols, the bundu treats us to a symphony, the cacophonous caroling of Christmas cicadas. These critters are ubiquitous. They fill every corner of the veldt with an ear-splitting screech, a rock concert decibel level that never eases for a minute. Mom says they will drive her crazy, but to me, it is the background noise of the bush. We learn to live with it.

Just before Christmas, Silas cuts down a scraggly mopane sapling. We prop it up on the verandah, decorate it with cotton balls and tinsel, and drape it with streamers made from popcorn or colored paper chains. Our decorations are plastic sprigs of the traditional mistletoe and holly that grace each doorway lintel.

Before eating Christmas dinner, we place a cracker on our plate. In this part of the world, Christmas crackers are not the same thing as American crackers, and neither are they edible. They are tubes made from paper and cardboard with a decorative exterior. When you pull them apart, one person gripping each end, they make a noise, a small, explosive *crack*—hence the name, "cracker." Inside are small, cheap gimcracks and paper crowns that we unfold and place on our heads.

Since we follow British traditions, "Santa" is known to us as "Father Christmas." We also celebrate Boxing Day, the day after Christmas, as a holiday. This tradition arose from the British custom when the rich gave the servants gifts, giving them a day off work. Although we are not rich, we have servants, and we honor this custom without knowing its origins.

Weeks before Christmas, Mom bakes a fruitcake and a plum pudding. Traditional Christmas fruitcake can remain fresh for years by the addition of brandy. The hard outer shell of almond marzipan and cement-like icing makes it impervious to penetration by any eating utensils, including our teeth. We all dislike it, yet the custom persists. Dentists probably love it, Dad says, since it must keep them quite busy.

The plum pudding does not contain a single plum, but, like the fruitcake, is a mix of raisins, citrus peel, and spices, preserved with brandy. It is served with a custard sauce or a lit brandy sauce brought flaming to the table. It is every bit as disgusting as the fruitcake, but we tolerate it for an obvious reason. As Mom makes the pudding, it is good luck for everyone to give it a stir, then she adds coins to the dessert and bakes it. The end result resembles a cannonball that has been passed through a furnace. It is Mom's baking, after all. We pick through the dark brown sludge on our plates, exclaiming in delight when we find a penny or a *tickey*. A tickey is a small silver coin worth three pennies, and these coins are usually all Mom can afford. The pudding remains mostly uneaten, joining the fruitcake of our Christmas celebration.

Our stockings are placed at the end of our beds and filled with oranges, small toys, or a Christmas cracker, while larger gifts are placed under the mopane sapling.

After we're put to bed on our first Christmas Eve at Buffalo Bend, I awaken from a deep sleep, disturbed by a small sound. I gaze around the dark room but don't see anything. I am about to turn over and go back to sleep when I glance at the window, blink, then rub my eyes. A large face, almost as big as the window, peers in at me. The face is unclear on this moonless night, a shadowy shape that seems to have a flat nose and a hood surrounding an oversize face. My hands fly to my mouth. I shiver with excitement. My heart leaps for joy: it is Father Christmas! It must be. Who else, I ask myself, would appear at our window in the middle of the night? Who else possesses a sleigh that can fly miles into the bushveld? We don't have a chimney, so he is probably looking for our forlorn mopane tree on our front verandah. I wonder if he can fit through the window—he looks enormous. But the doors aren't locked. Perhaps, I convince myself, he's just left our presents under our tree. I quickly snuggle back under the covers, close my eyes, and pretend I am asleep. When I dare open them again, the face is gone.

I feel honored to have seen Father Christmas. Butch and Rabbit will be so jealous. They've slept through it all.

The next morning, I run to the verandah, where we eagerly find our gifts under the tree. "Mom!" I yell, searching for my gift as she and Dad sleepily appear, still in their pajamas. "I saw Father Christmas last night!"

"Huh?" Mom rubs her eyes, frowning. Dad gives a half-smile, one that says he doesn't believe me.

"He came to the window. He brought us presents!" I insist, ripping off the colorful gift wrap and pull out—a new dress that Mom has sewn for me. Disappointed, I turn back to the tree, but no more gifts bear my name. Where is my gift from Father Christmas? I have written him letters, as early as November, telling him what I want. That is why he was at the window, wasn't it? He tried to let me know he'd delivered the doll I had asked for. I don't want any baby dolls. I want a grownup doll, like a Barbie. This is what I hoped he'd brought when I saw Father Christmas at the window. I persist, though. Surely the doll must be here, somewhere.

"I know he was here. He looked at me, Mom. I saw him! He had a big face, and I think he winked at me." I begin to embroider my vision as my mind fills in the blanks of the previous night's experience. "His eyes were blue, and he wore a red robe. He had a long, white beard, just like the pictures!"

Mom's eyebrows draw together, puzzled. She looks over at Dad, mouths something, and he gives a slight shake of his head and a small shrug.

Many years later, after I have learned the truth about Father Christmas, Mom lets me know it had not been a man at the window at all, not even Dad, but most likely a lion or other animal. They had not wanted to alarm us about our nocturnal visitor, preferring to indulge us in our Father Christmas myth.

We never have a lot of money to spend on gifts. Ours are usually practical, things we need, such as clothing, something handmade. We possess few toys or gadgets that other kids seem to have in plentiful supply. But the bush is our playground, and we find plenty to occupy us. A lack of gifts doesn't pose a problem for the local African kids, either. They make toys from items easily found in their world: little cars from scrap wire, dolls from corn cobs or fashioned from clay. We do the same. I love to play in the dirt, and clay figures are my favorite. I can sculpt almost anything out of the red, clay-like earth. I don't have time to get bored with the clay doll, either, since it holds together for about a day.

Even so, we look forward to Christmas, as hot and sweaty as it is. We long for the cold, white Christmases as depicted on the Christmas cards, but the closest we come to this is a *guti*, an African name for a soft, mist-like rain that often sets in at this time of year. It cools things off to the point where we can imagine it is snow—or even sleet—although we have no idea what that might feel or look like. Those who have fireplaces might use them, but since we don't have a fireplace, we wear our jerseys [cardigans] instead. We imagine the cotton balls on the tree to be real snow. However, more often than not, this time of the year is sultry and sizzling, making it difficult to put ourselves into scenes of snow and sleigh bells. Anyway, we do our best and observe all the northern hemisphere seasonal traditions as if they are the reality and our current environment is the dream.

We've made it through October. The rest of the year is a cinch.

Tea, Scones, and Malaria

CHAPTER 16

SCHOOL ON THE AIR

It is 1958, the year NASA is created. Although the space age has begun, it dawns on both Mom and Dad that their eldest is not rocket-scientist material. When it comes to arithmetic, my brain freezes into a solid block of congealed gray matter. I stare at the numbers on the page and wonder what they mean. Simple sums defeat me.

Mom despairs. "This child is so much like me," she wails to Dad after a particularly difficult arithmetic lesson. "She can't understand figures. How will she ever make it in life if she can't add or subtract?"

"You made it fine," Dad replies. "She's not going to need algebra or trigonometry, unless she has plans to take my job."

It is true. I never understand anything if it's related to science or figures. Looking at a column of numbers, or trying to decipher easy arithmetic posers such as, *if Johnny has 10 apples, and Sam has 15 and Jane takes 3 away from Johnny, how many...* make me weep, not to mention make my brain hurt. Reading, though, is my passion, as it is Mom's. By age seven, now in my second year of school, I discover Mom's "penny dreadfuls," books that young, impressionable minds should never read. Mom catches me reading one of these garishly covered books one day, and horrified, she snatches it out of my hands. "Can you even understand this?"

I nod, beaming. Of course. I love these books.

Mom obliges by buying me more suitable books on our monthly trips to town and stowing hers where she thinks I can no longer find them. She is wrong. I prefer adult books to the insipid kiddie stories of Dick and Jane, or Janet and John and their dog named Spot, or whatever these characters are called. Even though I don't understand much of what I read in Mom's books, I eagerly enunciate each word, trying to decipher the written codes that open up new worlds and horizons for me. Worlds that I one day will find and explore. Worlds far away from the bush and my boring life.

I consider the world I currently live in to be commonplace. It seems mundane, dull, compared to places like London, New York, and Paris. I genuinely have no idea just how unique my world or my childhood really is. In Nuanetsi, my only exposure to other makiwas is our nearest neighbors, American missionaries.

CHAPTER 17

MISSIONARIES

Our only white neighbors are Methodist missionaries, Americans, who live several hours away over rough roads. The Housers are dear friends, and we love to visit them on their sprawling mission. Tillman Houser is a tall man with gentle eyes. He has a smile that can light up a room, a mild demeanor, and is also a skilled storyteller. From Salem, Oregon, the strange and exotic tales of the farm he grew up on fascinate us. Auntie Gwen, his wife, is from South Dakota. She is a kind and motherly woman. Butch, Rabbit and I are both awed and terrified by their children, two boys who are older than us. We approach them with caution. They talk funny and dress different to most people. They wear brightly colored American shirts and blue jeans, things that are mostly unfamiliar to us.

"Hey, we won't bite you," one of them shouts. They laugh, but not in an unfriendly way. Nevertheless, Butch, Rabbit and I withdraw into the safety of the house. The adults are talking and Mom glares at us. "What are you doing inside?" she asks. "Counting teeth?" But Uncle Tillman's face brightens as we enter.

"Come here," he says, patting the sofa seat next to him, ignoring Mom. "I have another story for you!"

"About the barn?" I ask. I love the stories about his boyhood farm. "Tell us that one, again!"

He does. He tells us how his brother burned the barn down while playing with matches. A spasm of guilt ripples through me. Playing with matches is an old pastime of mine, although I've never burned anything down, yet. "Dad often took us behind the wood shed for a 'lickin','" he says with a chuckle, and I can also relate to that. We get a lot of lickin's too.

Even though it is a long drive over rough roads, we look forward to visiting them on their Methodist mission as often as possible. Auntie Gwen always has a hot meal waiting for us, and her cooking is much better than Mom's or Silas'. She has access to goodies mailed from the US, and there is always something special coming out of her kitchen, something we have never seen before. She gifts Mom with some beautiful American-made kitchenware; aluminum drinking glasses that shimmer metallically in rainbow colors, and a jug that completes the set. Mom treasures it and only takes them out for special occasions. These are not our every-day water glasses.

With friends like the Housers, bush life is made bearable, giving us a sense that we are not completely alone; that others, like us, have left the comforts of civilization behind to create a better world, whether building an infrastructure for our young country, or, in the case of these missionaries, assisting its inhabitants to enjoy a better life. The Housers understand the African concept that everything is connected because they, themselves, feel this connection to everything.

In later years, Tillman Houser writes his own memoirs, *Let Me Tell You...* I have not hesitated to use his real name in this memoir. He would have approved. I would like to share a quote from Uncle Tillman's memoir.

"I am so grateful to Africans who taught me to value and respect the extended family. Africans shared with me the basic concept that a person is really not an individual alone, but is made up of those who have gone before in this life as well as those who are living. They also taught me that each individual is important. Their world view is people-oriented rather than task-oriented. They highly value their language when spoken correctly. When an attempt is made to speak precisely it denotes that one cares for them."

Tillman Houser, *Let Me Tell You... A memoir.*

Tea, Scones, and Malaria

CHAPTER 18

THE HOSPITAL

Not all bush living is an endless picnic, though. Bush life has its drawbacks: a plethora of tropical diseases. Malaria is one, and following quickly on its heels comes the parasitical disease, bilharzia. I already know that the parasite lurks in stagnant water, but, at age seven, I just can't resist splashing through the shallow pools of the almost-dry riverbed.

Mom is pregnant and starting to show, but before Queenie is born, on one of our trips to Fort Victoria, she takes us to see the doctor for physical checkups and routine childhood immunization shots. I am also there for a nagging pain in my lower right abdomen. I've had some fever too. Butch and I enter the doctor's examination room with Mom first. The doctor examines me. "Hmm…," is all he says. He removes his stethoscope and gently prods my stomach. I wince. "Appendicitis. Probably bilharzia."

Mom's jaw tightens, her face paling.

"She needs her appendix out and quickly, before it bursts."

Do we all have this *bill* thing, I wonder, and what is an "appendix?" Is it my stomach? My heart skips some beats. I am about to die. *People who go to hospitals often don't come out,* I think, *especially if they lose a stomach. And how will I eat?* I look at

Butch, hot tears stinging my eyes. I wonder how she will manage without me. *What about Rabbit?* Tears flow freely now, but the doctor hands me a lollipop, and I forget about my impending death.

Rabbit is unimpressed when Butch and I emerge, each licking a lollipop. He can see my wet cheeks. He's not stupid. It is now his turn, and he is having none of it. He begins to whimper. He curls his legs around the chair legs and hooks his arms under the chair's arms. Mom tries to dislodge him and carry him into the doctor's examination room, but for a four-year-old, he has the strength of Atlas. The receptionist, an older lady, tries to help Mom, but Rabbit only screams louder, and, short of breaking his legs, they cannot pry him off the chair. The doctor emerges from his exam room.

"What's going on here?"

Mom explains, but isn't it obvious?

The doctor joins the two of them trying to pry Rabbit's fingers from the armrest, but as soon as they get a hand loose, he tightens his leg grip. With a sigh, the doctor picks up the chair with Rabbit still in it and carries him into the exam room. Butch and I chuckle as Rabbit's screams penetrate the closed door, but eventually, Rabbit gets his shots and the lollipop.

A few days later, I am admitted to the local hospital, a low, red-roofed, white-washed building surrounded by tall, shady gum trees. The surgeon removes my appendix, and I spend a further two weeks in the hospital receiving the bilharzia treatment. I no longer remember what the treatment was. The children's ward is a bright and airy room of about five beds. I am the only person in the ward until a young boy who has just had his tonsils removed joins me. We share books and toys, and I often read to him from my *Ollie Ostrich* black and white picture book. I explain to him how my grandmother had once taken care of ostriches and had even been kicked by one. This seems to impress the boy. "Wow. I wish I had an ostrich!"

"Me too," I agree. "Everyone would be so jealous and would wish they could have one, too." I color Ollie Ostrich purple with a crayon. He is my favorite character. No one messes with him.

The boy soon leaves, though, and I return to solitary confinement.

A screened-in verandah runs the full length of the building. This is where I sit every day reading my age-appropriate books—Mom is taking no chances here—or playing with the toys I have been given. It is the first time I can recall that I have so many toys and books. I never tire of the jewelry set with its colorful glass beads that I make into charms and bracelets to gift to Mom and Butch.

My surgeon, Dr. Sykes, is also a local practitioner, but not the same genial doctor I had previously seen. He reminds me of a cigarette butt. He is like the unfiltered *Star* cigarettes Oupa flicks out into the yard just before they burn his nicotine-stained fingers. Short and squat on the outside, Dr. Sykes burns red-hot inside. He can be charming and gracious one moment, and the next, he morphs into a rabid dog. A few days after my surgery, he and two nurses arrive to change my surgical dressing. Without taking any time to prepare me for possible discomfort, he rips the adhesive tape from my tender belly. It is a few seconds of excruciating pain that catches me unaware, so I cry out.

To the two nurses' shock, Dr. Sykes' face turns beet-red, and a stream of curses tumble out of his mouth. He uses words I've never heard from my parents or anyone else, not even my drunken grandfather, and a lot of them begin with "f." I begin to sob as his foul words hit me like a barrage of bricks and arrows. He rounds off his diatribe to tell me to shut up, to stop crying, as he rips off more of the tape. But the more I cry, the more he curses, and the more he curses, the more I cry.

The nurses freeze, horror and disgust etched into their faces. Still, it is apparent they have no intention of intervening. They are as afraid of this doctor as I am. This happens almost daily, every time my dressing needs changing. Unsurprisingly, I grow to fear doctors in general. Many years later, other doctors who have seen my appendix scar ask me who was responsible for the shark bite on my stomach. The incision is abnormally large and jagged, a permanent memento of Dr. Sykes. Some years later, we belatedly learn Dr. Sykes does have a problem: a drug problem. It explains much of his behavior.

The nurses at this hospital make up for Dr. Sykes, though. They treat me as if I am the only patient in the hospital and do their best to make me feel comfortable during a long convalescence that drags into infinity. It does end eventually, and I am overjoyed to see Mom and Dad's faces when they finally come to pick me up and take me home.

The bush life has infected my psyche as if it were bilharzia or malaria. It is only here where I know true freedom, where I am not confronted by makiwas who frighten me, and where no-one cares how I dress. When I am away from Buffalo Bend, I am forced to be a civilized child, to wear shoes, to wash my face when I get up in the morning, instead of just jumping out of bed, throwing on a dress, and running barefoot down to the river before breakfast. Makiwas always want other makiwas to dress as if we are in London or Paris. I don't like it. Mom and Petina never make us do all these things unless we're going to Fort Victoria, or to see the doctor, or visit friends. Even School on the Air doesn't care if I haven't washed my face or brushed my teeth.

It becomes evident to me that Mom is pregnant again, and it is not an easy one. She becomes too stressed to continue teaching me. One day in December she sits me down in one of our gaily cushioned verandah chairs and places a plate of her jam tarts on the coffee table. She never messes these up. They are always delicious. Butch and Rabbit are taking an afternoon nap. Petina sits nearby, giving me a sideways stare as if she knows something I do not. I feel honored, though — privileged — to be the only one who has been offered jam tarts. And all before dinner, too! I eagerly help myself to one after determining which appears to be the biggest.

Mom clears her throat, a phony smile plastered on her face. "Would you like to go to a real school?" Her voice sounds fake-happy, but I am too busy licking the jam out of the tart to notice. I just nod and quickly take another tart before she changes her mind. She hasn't even asked me to wash my hands, and they are still brown with outside dirt.

"We have enrolled you at a school in Gwelo," she continues, her fake smile fixed now. "It's a boarding school, and it's run by our church."

I look up; a jam tart still clutched in my hand. "School? Church?" A dark cloud passes over the sun, and I blink.

"Yes. Dad and I think it's best for you, Pie. I can't teach you anymore. You need a good education, and with Butch, Rabbit, and another baby coming, things are..." She shrugs, her eyes searching the rafters for an answer I would understand. "Busy."

"Okay," I say and shove the tart inside my mouth, chewing. "Ish fine." But I'm not sure. There will only be more makiwa's to deal with.

Mom gives a tight smile, a relieved sigh as she rises, frowning at my dirty hand. "Good. We'll be leaving in a few weeks. The school year begins in January. Don't eat them all at once."

I am still only seven. I am due to start as a boarder at the beginning of the school year, in January 1958.

After I finish off the plate of tarts, I sit for a while, thinking. I have mixed feelings about going away to school. On the one hand, I dread it, but I am also excited, eager to experience new things. If Mom is too busy to teach, then I am willing. *But*, I think, *will I have to wear shoes all the time?*

Little do I know what awaits me at this school.

CHAPTER 19

BOARDING SCHOOL

1958

From an idyllic, stress-free life in the bush, I transition to one taken from the pages of *Oliver Twist*. I am propelled into a Gothic realm that seems more suited to that of the Dark Ages. When my parents drop me off at this school, I remember it as the worst day of my life, going from anticipation to dread in a few hours. I convince myself while en route to the school that my parents no longer want me.

We have no sooner left Nuanetsi than I begin to have misgivings. *What does it mean that Mom is too busy? She has Petina. Petina can take care of the others while Mom teaches me. She does this anyway.* The harsh reality is beginning to sink into my jam-tart-addled brain. Plenty of other moms teach their children all over the country. Why not me? *Is it because...?* I begin to think of all the bad things I've done in the past few months, such as the time I found Mom's bar of Cadbury's with nuts under her pillow. I ate it all. Maybe... it is the time when I read one of Mom's penny-dreadful picture books with pictures that made her shriek and grab the book from my hands... I continue in this vein of thought for a while.

"Mom, Dad. I don't want to go," I announce in the car as we approach Fort Vic.

Dad grimaces. "You're going. We've decided. It's too late to back out now, anyway."

Mom sits in the front seat and doesn't look at me. I can see her shoulders shaking. Is she laughing? I begin to sob. Dad sighs. Mom's shoulders shake some more and I hear sniffing. Now I know. They don't want me anymore. I'll never see them again. I cry all the way to Gwelo, howling, heart-rending sobs. I know now, without any doubt, that I should never have agreed to this insane idea. I hadn't realized just how far away this school is. The trip seems to take forever, but at last we arrive. We drive through the iron gate onto a spreading campus surrounded by fences and fields. Mom wipes my tear-streaked face with her handkerchief as we climb out of the Land Rover.

A jovial looking man emerges from a small building to greet us. Mom's face is artificially bright and cheery, but her gray eyes glint with unshed tears. "Say hello to your new headmaster, Mr. Bumble," she says.

I hide behind Mom's skirt, looking up at this man with his curly mop of fair hair, big smile, and twinkling blue eyes.

"Welcome!" He sticks out a meaty hand, and Mom and Dad shake hands with him. "She'll be very happy here, and unlike government schools, we'll make sure she gets a good Christian education. You won't be sorry," he adds, as he escorts us from building to building, waving his arms as he describes each one.

The classrooms are all in one long ground-level building, a total of about six for each "standard," which is the equivalent of an American grade. It is a co-ed primary school, ages seven through twelve.

"We keep strict standards at our school," Mr. Bumble explains. "None of this government school laxness. We don't spare the rod, here, either."

Dad nods his approval, and I feel Mom's slight, inward cringe as she clasps my hand tighter. With its modest, squat buildings spread out over a tract of land, the school is surrounded on all sides by veldt. It is a different kind of veldt here than what I am used to: savannah grassland dotted with clumps of tall trees and low kopjes in the distance.

The girl's dormitory, where I will be housed, is close to the classrooms. On one end is the older girl's dorm, then the younger girl's dorm, and at the end nearest the classrooms is the bathroom. The concrete floors are cold and unwelcoming. In places, they are cracked and sunken. Bunk beds line the walls, and everything smells of mold.

Mom and Dad leave me in the hands of the matron, a motherly woman who takes me to her quarters and gives me a cookie. I love her immediately. I stop crying and soon settle in with the other girls, but I feel as if I have been abandoned. The school, with the exception of our matron, does nothing to disabuse me of this notion.

Mr. Bumble, at first glance, appears to be a kind Christian man. Mom and Dad admire him, and he is also an old family friend. I surmise later that Mom and Dad trusted this man to give me an education that will reflect their own morals and beliefs. Their fear of government-run schools overwhelms their common sense. To them, government schools are hotbeds of sin and iniquity. It doesn't take long for me to realize that Mr. Bumble uses physical punishment threats against the students to keep them in line. I am never thrashed by him, he always treats me well, but I live in fear of being summoned to his home to receive "cuts." Cuts are just what the word sounds like—a whipping with a cane on the rear end that causes red welts. It is a barbaric, cruel, and perverted custom, a hold-over from the Victorian era. Our principal uses it more on the boys, but some girls tell me stories about being on the receiving end.

The woman who runs the kitchen and dining room is the principal's wife, Mrs. Bumble, a gray-haired woman with intense eyes and thin lips.

The people who run the school do not eat meat. They are vegetarians, but I am accustomed to meat. If the food had been even slightly palatable, perhaps I could have thrived on vegetarianism. Instead, it is tasteless and unappetizing slop. They serve us the cheapest food money can buy—thick mealie-meal mush (cornmeal) in which lurk worms. Not the crunchy caterpillars of the bush, but tiny, pale, maggoty things that do nothing for the appetite. We eat few eggs, so our protein is limited. We are served mostly carbohydrates with overcooked vegetables and no seasoning. Our mid-morning treat is sugary Kool-Aid. It reminds me of our deworming medicine. In winter, it is chocolate-flavored Milo, which I actually like.

One meal stands out in my memory. It is lunch, and we are served spaghetti with tomato sauce. Usually, I love pasta, but the spaghetti is cooked to a gluey mound. The watery sauce it swims in, in no way resembles anything that looks or tastes like tomatoes, looking instead like a pile of pink worms squirming on my plate. I have seen the same thing many times in the bush, usually on a dead animal. I take one bite and retch. My tablemates are eating it up as if it is haute cuisine from a Michelin restaurant. Mrs. Bumble notices that I am not eating and sidles over to our table. One of the rules of the dining room is that no one can leave until everyone finishes eating.

"You're not leaving until you finish eating," she says, "Every bit of it. Even if you sit here all day." She returns to her station and makes the announcement. No one is to leave until I have finished every scrap on my plate.

I sit with my arms folded while Mrs. Bumble stares at me from across the room. The teachers can't leave, either. No one can go — I have not finished. My tablemates and the kids in the dining room glare at me. They try to coax me into eating, but I am not going to eat that stuff. Strangely, we've been served worse, and as nauseating as this slop is, I've eaten even more of their disgusting meals without complaint. Somewhere in my background, though, my Italian DNA rises to the surface. It informs me that it is an act of betrayal to a Venetian great-grandfather to eat this spaghetti dish.

Around two p.m., Mrs. Bumble, tiring of our battle of wills, excuses my table and the other kids and teachers. Another hour passes. I can tell she is weakening. I am the girl who once hid, silent and without moving, behind a sofa all day. She has no idea who she is dealing with. We are the only two left in the dining room. The workers have cleaned up and gone home. The uneaten dish now resembles something from a science experiment gone wrong. It sits cold and congealed on my plate.

At last, with a sigh and a toss of her head, Mrs. Bumble indicates I should leave. It is my small victory. I would have sat there until dinner time if I'd had to.

I miss my family. I miss the bush. I crave meat and would sell my soul for a steak pie or a lamb chop. I cry myself to sleep every night, and on many occasions, I wet the bed. I have never been a bed-wetter before.

I have a recurring dream that I can still recall. I have escaped from the school. I run down the road as fast as my legs can carry me, but every time I reach a certain point, a black car pulls up alongside. It is Mr. Bumble. He opens the door and forces me into the car. His cane sits on the seat next to me. It is at that point I wake up and discover I am still at school, and my bed is wet.

I am already a skinny child before coming to this place, but here I wither away to a skeletal frame. Our visiting government nurse grows concerned after she weighs me. She calls in a doctor who examines me. Later, I hear from my parents that the doctor has written a letter to the principal to ensure we get more protein. For a while, we eat eggs one or two days a week. There is some improvement in the menu, and then it all slides back to the status quo: maggoty porridge and bread—a lot of bread—so we'll fill up and not complain. However, I never fill up. The gnawing hunger I experience here is intense and unceasing.

One day, as I am brushing my teeth at the bathroom sink, my stomach growling with hunger, I look down at the tube of toothpaste in my hand. After rinsing, I squeeze a small amount onto my finger, put it in my mouth, and swallow. It doesn't taste good at all, but I imagine I am eating peppermints. Squeezing out another lump, I lick at it eagerly until I have eaten nearly half the tube. It is just as I am about to squeeze the tube again that it is snatched from my hand by one of the older girls who has silently crept up behind me.

"What are you doing?" she shrieks. "Oh my God. You didn't...I am going to tell the matron, and she'll tell Mr. Bumble! You're in trouble. You're going to get cuts!" She turns on her heel and storms out of the bathroom.

I run outside the bathroom door to my favorite place, under a guava tree. The tree's branches hang low to the ground, creating a small space where my friends and I play. I feel safe here and sit, trembling, as tears run down my face. I am too afraid to go to class, but an older girl is sent to find me and haul me into the classroom. I feel as if every eye is on me: *the toothpaste eater*! After school, a bunch of older girls gather around me, taunting. Their jibes and jeers, predictions of what Mr. Bumble will do to me for eating toothpaste, are much worse than a physical beating. Soon, they promise, I will be summoned to Mr. Bumble's home for a whipping that I will never forget, and it will teach me that I should never eat toothpaste again.

The call never comes. No one ever mentions the toothpaste incident to me again, and I suffer no ill effects from eating half a tube of unnatural, possibly toxic chemicals.

I receive news from home that I am a big sister once again. In June 1958, baby Queenie is born. Mom and Dad bring her to the school for me to see, and I learn how to change a diaper. It is pretty disgusting, I think, but I am proud I can master it and feel quite grown-up. I wish I could go home to be with my baby sister. I beg, "I'll be good! I'll help with Queenie!" I watch, tears pouring down my cheeks, as the car heads out of the front gate, and then turns onto the road to Fort Victoria. I run to the gate, climbing on top of the brick gate pillar, and keep watch until the car disappears into the distance.

I survive a year at this school. For the first time in my life, I become acquainted with a new-to-me reality called "winter." Due to the savannah's altitude and flatness, the weather is pleasant and mild in the summer but frigid in the winter months. The biting wind roars and howls, unobstructed, across the flat expanse. Our classroom building is sheltered on one side, but as I round its corner, a blast of frigid air almost knocks me off my feet. The birdbath outside freezes overnight, and we shiver under our thin blankets in the unheated dormitory. Since I've always lived in a hot climate, I have no winter clothing. We are always cold, and I develop chilblains on my fingers. I hold my hands under hot, running water to warm them up, but that only makes the chilblains worse.

The doctor visits again. He writes a letter to my parents, telling them to remove me from this school. At the end of that year, I return home, this time for good. Mom and Dad tell me many years later they always regretted sending me to this school, but now it doesn't matter anymore. We are moving again, this time, to Fort Victoria.

PART II

CIVILIZATION AND MY TRIBE

1959—1963

Tea, Scones, and Malaria

CHAPTER 20

A DUCKTAIL

1959

At the end of 1958 I return home to Buffalo Bend for Christmas, having endured my last miserable day at the boarding school. Mom and Dad are taking the doctor's recommendations seriously. In the new year, the year I turn nine, Jonas Salk creates a vaccine for polio. Around the world the vaccine becomes a game-changer. I am to attend a government school in January, and I will be vaccinated there, Mom tells me. It is a relief for them. Polio is always on their minds thanks to graphic news reports showing children in iron lungs or walking on crutches. While on another trip to Fort Vic, Mom and Dad take us to see a movie, *The Five Pennies*, with Danny Kaye, a movie about polio. We all cry when the character's young daughter contracts polio. I think it is real, and that we'll all get polio too, but now, thanks to Dr. Salk, Mom tells us we won't be in any danger from that disease.

Dad has finished the bridge, but the end of the job also means the end of our sojourn at Buffalo Bend. Blackie, our semi-feral cat, has long since disappeared, and we've lost Fritz to a snake bite. Silas has moved on to other prospects, so we are only taking Petina with us.

Petina is as excited as we are. "*Ay!* I go to the big city!" Petina has never left Nuanetsi, and the outside world is alien to her. She only hears our stories of the town we go to once a month to restock on supplies.

"It's not a big city, Petina," Mom says, "but it's not the bush life for us anymore."

As thrilling as our new prospects are, we are all sad to leave the bush. I have no idea what town life will be like. Fort Victoria is bigger than Zaka. I've been to Fort Victoria many times before and it seems a pleasant place. It sits midway between the Lowveld and the Highveld and is the oldest town in the country, the first place the pioneer column settled on its way up from South Africa in 1890.

Its paved streets are broad, lined with colorful jacaranda and flamboyant trees. The feathery-leafed jacaranda blooms in spring, creating a colorful show of purple trumpet-shaped blossoms that carpet roads and sidewalks, making walking slippery and treacherous. The flamboyant, or flame tree, with its orange-red flowers puts on a show, dropping flowers and long, flat seed pods onto the ground that we gather for sword play and the flowers for garland-making.

The central Bell Tower looms over Main Street, opposite the Civic Center with its green, parklike setting. The original purpose of the rectangular tower, built of farm bricks in 1890, was intended to ring curfew. King Lobengula of the Matabele was understandably incensed when the pioneers occupied Mashonaland, and he threatened to attack the town. The pioneers responded by banning all people from the streets between 6 p.m. and 6 a.m., but in my time, there is no curfew.

On one side of the wide main street, Meikles, the town's only department store, with its enormous green awnings, dominates the town's center. Meikles occupies two buildings: its grocery store is in an older building with white concrete pillars and a tin-roofed verandah, while the department store sits next to it in a newer corner building. Next to Meikles is a garage. Stretching across the establishment's prominent concrete panel is the name "Duly's Co. Ltd." This is where everyone takes their vehicles to be fixed or to fill up. The main street is wide enough for a central island of feathery date palms and small shrubs.

Fort Victoria is also a jumping-off place for tourism to the famous Zimbabwe Ruins—a stone ruin located about 30 miles from the town, an enigmatic collection of stone edifices built centuries ago and shrouded in mystery and legend. It is where the country got its current name, and it has graced many a postage stamp or tourist leaflet for the country.

Surrounded by green kopjes and sprawling savannah, Fort Vic—as we call it—is also a pretty town, but the best thing about it is that there are government-run day schools. I no longer need to go to boarding school or be homeschooled. There is a kindergarten, which Butch and Rabbit attend, while I, now nine years old, attend the junior (middle) school. Petina stays busy taking care of baby Queenie while Mom works in her new job as an administrative assistant to the owner of the local bakery.

The first house we rent is in the older part of town, a duplex, single level home with another family living in the other half: a hard-drinking couple who always have an open beer in their hands. They have a sixteen-year-old son named Dustin.

Our half of the house smells musty, the sourness of age and damp. It is also one of the spookiest houses I have ever lived in. I am uneasy in this house with its creaking floorboards and gloomy, foreboding rooms. The pantry is so dark Dad says we can grow mushrooms in it. We go in there and shut the door and make up spooky stories. We play a game to see who can stay in there the longest without screaming or running out. The game never lasts too long. The property has a depressing aura: a black hole where light cannot penetrate. The house terrifies me.

Although in the middle of town, the home is not hooked up to the sewage system. We are forced, once again, to venture outside to an outhouse. This outhouse, though, is luxurious by our previous standards. Despite not being equipped with electricity, the sturdy walls and a door that one can latch gives us a sense of privacy and safety. There is a plentiful supply of magazines and mail-order catalogs piled on the wide wooden seat. The outhouse is the one place where the dark aura of the house does not penetrate. Whenever nature calls, I take the flashlight and pore over the catalogs, imagining I am picking out anything I want and that it will magically appear in front of me. The toilet is my refuge, a welcoming respite from the house. I spend a lot of time here. I avidly read the Hollywood star magazines our neighbors who live in the other half have left behind. For the first time in my life, I hear about movies and movie stars. Until now, I have not even known of their existence, and my world begins to expand.

Katlynn Brooke

I am awed by Dustin, the neighbor's red-headed teenage son. Other than the two American missionary boys, I have never seen anyone like him before. Dustin wears his hair in a "ducktail," a pomaded, slicked back hairstyle that comes to a Vee in the back, rising in the nape of the neck to what looks like a duck's ass. This style is the rage in the Fifties for disaffected teenagers. To complete the stereotypical 50s teen image, he also wears a leather bomber jacket. I think he is so hip. Dustin and I never speak. He tolerates my presence as I sit on the verandah, where he hangs out, and I stare at him as he plays scratchy records on a portable gramophone.

To Dad, though, boys or men who wear this hairstyle are "ducktails," lowlifes, Rock 'n Rollers who are not worthy of coming anywhere near his daughters. He forbids me to go out onto the verandah when Dustin is home, but I regularly disobey this order. At this time, though, I am only nine years old, so it seems unlikely Dustin would be even remotely interested. Dad, both at this time of my life and later in my teens, is under the illusion that he must protect me from boys. He mistakenly tends to see me with my freckles, missing teeth, skinny legs, and mousy brown hair as someone I am not. I am not a girl who needs to beat boys off with a stick. His fears are unfounded. Dustin, or other boys, never give me a second glance.

Instead, Dustin is obsessed with Elvis Presley. Although he is a rabid fan, Dustin only possesses a single Elvis record, a 45 rpm; *Jailhouse Rock*. The boy plays this record repeatedly. After he comes home from school, he places *Jailhouse Rock* on the turntable of his portable record player. Each time the song finishes, he raises the stylus and replays it, over and over. Like a Christmas cicada, he never wearies.

Mom and Dad are losing their minds. Dad darkly plots to smash the gramophone and the record into tiny pieces. Instead, they complain to his parents. They do nothing. They have no doubt imbibed themselves into insensibility years ago, but Mom and Dad's central nervous systems are still intact. Finally, Dad has had enough of *Jailhouse Rock*, and he locates another rental in town.

CHAPTER 21

NIKI, SPORTS, AND *BEANOS*

1959-1960

My first day at junior school at age nine is as frightening to me as my first day at the boarding school. I know no-one. The kids ignore me. I stand on the verandah at break, watching them play in the quadrangle, a central square surrounded by classrooms. I feel alone and left out, too shy to force my way into groups who all seem to know each other. Nearby, a dark-haired girl grips a verandah support pole as if it were her mother and stares at me with sad brown eyes. I am bracing myself for something — I am not sure what. My breath catches in my throat as she lets go of the pole and approaches. She stops in front of me and stares directly, pleadingly, into my face.

"Will you be my friend?"

I heave a sigh of relief. "Yes. What is your name?"

"Niki. It's my first day here, and I don't know anyone."

Niki is Greek, and she is as shy as I am. It is surprising that she even found the courage to ask me to be her friend. I am pleased to discover Niki and I are alike in many ways: we both love comics, hate school sports, and she, too, cannot grasp science and arithmetic, but for some reason, she thinks I am better at arithmetic than she is. We must write down the answers during mental arithmetic tests as the teacher calls out the problem. We sit together, and Niki's breath comes in panicked gasps. I am still pondering the answer to a problem called three questions ago.

Niki elbows me. "Psst! I need to copy from you. I'm too far behind to catch up."

I shrug, turning my exercise book slightly. It's no use, and we know it. We both do poorly in this subject, and neither of us ever improves.

While I am a string bean, Niki remains stubbornly on the chubby side. We dread school sports. Rounders, a game like softball, is an after-school activity in which we are both forced to participate. We are always picked last for teams, and kids groan when Niki and I are assigned to their team. I grasp the bat, squinch my eyes shut as the ball is lobbed toward me, then swinging wildly, I throw the bat away and scurry toward first base. I rarely make it before the kid on the base catches a leisurely tossed ball and yells, "Out!" Niki does little better, and we spend the rest of the game sitting on the sidelines, where we feel we belong.

Tennis is a game that neither of us excels in, either. Invariably, we are assigned to the practice wall, safely isolated from those kids with promise. I turn my ankle regularly just running for the ball. I wrench my wrist when I finally manage to hit it with the heavy racket Mom has loaned me from her tennis-playing days in the Forties.

"I can't help that I have weak ankles and wrists," I moan to Niki, who is staring at the sky as she twirls her racket tip on the clay surface. Her balls lie, forgotten, in the weeds near the court fence.

"I hate this. I want to go home," she says. "I have a new *Beano*."

I am envious. Niki's Mom gives her money for comics, and she has a collection that astonishes me. We spend many lazy afternoons reading comics as we listen to Elvis records on her portable player. Like Dustin, Niki is an Elvis fan.

"Stop faffing around!" Mr. Styles, the tennis coach, yells at us from the next court. I want to see you hitting those balls. C'mon now!"

I don't think I'll ever love tennis.

Our new rental home on Robertson Street is within walking distance of our school, near the center of town. The house is typical of homes in this area: an old brick bungalow with a tin roof, a small front porch, servant's quarters in the rear, and a garage. It has an indoor bathroom equipped with full plumbing, electricity, and hot and cold running water. Scarlet bougainvillea blooms in clusters around the yard and a patch of lawn flourishes in front of the house. It is the first lawn we've ever had.

A convenience store on the corner of our street caters to our new addiction to sweets, as candy is called here. It is the reason my siblings and I never have tithe money for the church. Restraint is not one of our strengths, and the church is dangerously close to the corner store. Butch, Rabbit, and I slip out of the service before the offering plate is passed around and make a quick run to the store. We return before anyone notices we are missing, and no one ever notices we are a little short on the offering.

We seldom, if ever, receive pocket money to do with as we please. When we do get a few tickeys or sixpences, it is because we've washed Mom's car or weeded the garden. Cleaning up our rooms does not earn us extra. Mom believes strongly that we should give any money we make to the church, and like the widow's mite, she always has tithe money.

Sometimes, I save my coins to buy comics instead of sweets. The bookstore, Belmont Press, has an eye-popping selection of children's comics: Marvel and Action Comics, and my favorites, the British comics *Beano* and *The Dandy*. I would kill for a *Beano*, with its Bash Street Kids, Lord Snooty and his pals, Windbag.... I know all the comic characters intimately. Plug of the Bash Street Kids is my hero. They all embody my sense of mischievous humor.

While the boys, including Rabbit, crouch behind the magazine stand, giggling as they thumb through the girlie magazines, Niki and I kneel on the floor, reading *Beano*. The giggles and snorts coming from behind the stands, though, alert the sales clerk to our presence. She stalks over with a harrumph, and with arms folded, orders us out of the store — immediately. "And return the comics and magazines exactly to where you found them!" Chastened, we leave, but as soon as we notice the clerk busying herself with a customer through the store window, we sneak back in. It becomes a game of sorts to enter undetected or see how long we can remain before she chases us out again. Sometimes, though, I may have enough coins to pay for a comic, and the sales clerk frowns at me over her spectacles as she rings up my illicit purchase. She knows how many freebies I have already read from cover to cover.

Everything is within walking distance for us, including our church and Main Street, with its bigger shops. This is a new situation for me. We are no longer country bumpkins. I feel cosmopolitan, like my hero Superman from the comics, a dweller in the city of Metropolis. Well, if not quite Metropolis, we at least have neighbors.

The Joneses, our neighbors, are Ozzie and Harriet, who have well-adjusted children our age, unlike the neighbors on our other side, whose kids throw stones at us. They look like snooty types and always wear nice clothes. Unlike us, we never see them dirty or barefoot. We play with the Jones kids instead of the rock-throwers, and go swimming at the town pool with Niki. The town pool is our other treat. It is Olympic size with grassy areas to sunbathe, changing rooms, and high diving boards. One of the Jones family girls eventually becomes a champion diver and swimmer. I watch as she does swan dives from the high diving board, envious and awed at the same time. I venture up onto the diving board once or twice, but as soon as I get to the end, I sink down to my knees, defeated, and crawl back, my legs shaking. Niki doesn't notice. She is asleep on her towel under a large shade tree with a *Beano* over her face.

It is at this pool where I learn to swim. An older boy throws me into the deep end and leaves me to sink or swim.

There are no lifeguards at our pool, and if one drowns here, it may be a few weeks before anyone knows. After flailing around for a bit, coughing and sputtering as I swallow water, I get the hang of it. I paddle to the side, grabbing onto the edge like a limpet before making my way back to the shallow end. I have previously bathed in the ocean and rivers, but the pool is deeper than the areas where I venture in the sea or river. I gradually lose my fear, though, and learn how to dog-paddle my way around the swimming pool.

Mom's job at the bakery ends, and she takes a better-paying job as secretary to the manager of Meikles. Dad returns to the bush again, only coming home on weekends. I think my boarding school experience has shaken them to the core, and they decide to do what is best for us by leaving us in town. Bush living with school-age children is not practical, and I am not their only school-age child to worry about.

Despite my friendship with Niki, I have a difficult time at the government school. My previous schooling has left me with scars on my psyche. I am a trembling mess, expecting punishment from every quarter. Life will give me what I expect and much sooner than I think.

CHAPTER 22

MISS NETTLES

1960-1961

Miss Nettles, a tall, gray-haired, bony woman who reminds me of a scarecrow, teaches my nature study class every Friday. When she looks my way, her eyes pin me down as if I am an insect on a collection board. Nature study has the potential to be one of my favorite subjects, because it is a subject that I know well. Once I get to know Miss Nettles, though, it turns into my least favorite subject.

One Friday, Barbara, a girl who sits at the desk next to me, blinks, shakes her head and turns to me. "I can't see the board," she whispers. "I left my glasses at home. May I copy from your notes?"

I nod and push my notes around so she can see them. I can't see why not. It isn't a test or an exam, just copying stuff that Miss Nettles has written from the blackboard into our notebooks. I don't realize how wrong I am. Miss Nettles, her cobra eyes alighting on Barbara, slowly places the chalk down and picks up a ruler from her desk. Barbara has not noticed. She is still looking at my notebook while writing furiously. Miss Nettles leisurely strolls down our aisle, slapping her ruler against one hand.

Smack, smack! She takes several steps closer, her eyes fixed on Barbara. I can't breathe. My knees begin to knock together. Barbara, still unaware of the approaching danger, keeps writing. Miss Nettles draws closer. *Smack, smack!*

Please, please, please, God make her keep going, I beg an uncaring deity, who seems to be deaf as well. I can't take my eyes off Miss Nettles. The rest of the class, now aware of the approaching terror, freezes. I now know how mice must feel when confronted with a cobra. She stops. She has reached our desk. God is definitely not listening. She pulls both our textbooks toward her, looking down, comparing our notes.

"You are cheating." It's more a statement than a question. It must have escaped her sharp eye that these identical notes are written in chalk on the board, but I don't dare say that out loud. I sit there as if I have been turned to stone, unable to speak or move.

Barbara's face is ashen. "N-no Miss. I can't see what you're writing on the board," her voice emerges as a terrified squeak.

"You're cheating!" Miss Nettles spits. She jerks Barbara up by her ear, yanks up her skirt, giving the class a good look at poor Barbara's panties. With a smirk that tells me I'll be next, Miss Nettles delivers a series of stinging thwacks on the girl's bare thigh with the ruler. A hush descends on the room as twenty or so terrified students gape and shrink down in their seats. Then it is my turn, and I receive the same treatment as my classmate. It is not so much painful as humiliating, although I bear red marks for a while after on my leg. I never tell Mom or Dad. I am afraid Dad will come to the school and raise a ruckus, or perhaps worse. When Dad gets angry, his face turns red, and his eyes bulge. He often threatens, to no one in particular, to shoot people who make him angry. No one ever takes him seriously. We see it as mostly bluster, but I am not taking any chances.

Instead, my solution to this problem is to pretend I am sick. Every. Single. Friday. Mom is a pushover. She allows me to stay home when I fake illness. It is usually a "stomach ache" or a "headache." The migraines, to which both of us are susceptible, come in handy, and bolster my headache claim. Mom anxiously brings out the thermometer.

"You don't have a temperature."

"But Mom, I feel sick. My head hurts, and my tummy too."

Mom isn't sure. Migraines don't spike a temperature. She pokes my tummy, stares at me anxiously, and shakes her head. Mom always believes me when I say I am sick. I don't know why. "Alright, but I must go to work, and Petina can't take care of you. I'll ask Mrs. Jones if you can come over to her house. She'll keep an eye on you."

Mrs. Jones always agrees. She tucks me into one of her children's beds and brings me soup or a sandwich, which I still eat, no matter how bad my "stomach ache." When Mom comes home from work, I am sent home. Mrs. Jones is not fooled, though. She talks to Mom and Dad. She asks them why I am sick only on Friday's yet can still eat like a horse, and in the afternoons, after school is over, I am observed running around with the other kids. Dad knows immediately that something is up, and he isn't going to stand for it.

One Friday, Dad "happens" to be home when I pull this stunt. I have no sooner mentioned my stomach ache when he rises from the breakfast table, a dark and dangerous look on his face.

"Get in the car. Now." He drags me, sobbing, to the car. Yelling at me all the way, we drive the short distance to school, where he marches me, unannounced, into the Headmaster's office.

"I want to see Mr. Winston, immediately," he demands of the aghast secretary.

"I-er, he's busy right now. Why don't you make an appointment...?"

"I said *now*." Dad's cheeks are flushed, and I continue to wail at a volume that must penetrate Mr. Winston's office's closed door. He pokes his head out.

"What seems to be the problem?"

"I want to know why my child doesn't want to come to school on Fridays," Dad demands.

"Come on in." Mr. Winston opens his office door wider and ushers us in.

Mr. Winston is a trim, genial man with graying hair. After we are seated in front of his desk, he cocks his head, giving me a quizzical look. "Why don't you want to come to school on Fridays?"

I can't look at him. I can't speak, I am still sobbing, and my knees shake. My lips are shut tighter than a bank vault, and no matter how much they grill me, I refuse to talk. Mr.

Winston shrugs. "I'll keep an eye on her," he promises, and Dad leaves. I am sent to class, but I feel sure that Miss Nettles will somehow find out about Dad's visit. Dad has no idea why I won't go to school on Fridays, but I feel sure he suspects it is because I have not studied or done my homework. It makes him angry.

Not long after the episode with Dad, one particularly frigid winter morning, Miss Nettles singles me out for special attention. I go to school wearing a red cardigan. Our school uniform demands a blue sweater or cardigan. Mom has not yet had time to get me one per school regulations. She doesn't have enough money for a new cardigan and instead has decided to knit one for me, but it is not yet finished. I feel Miss Nettles' cold eye on me, a coiling black mamba getting ready to strike, as I walk down the long, open-sided verandah to my classroom. I draw closer, my head down, heart pounding.

The mamba strikes. With a quick movement, she grabs my ear, twisting as she pulls me closer.

"Where is your school cardigan?" she hisses. It seems to me a reptilian tongue flicks in and out of her mouth, but I think she is licking her lips.

"My mother hasn't knitted it for me yet."

"Go home now, and don't return until you have the cardigan." She gives my ear an extra twist before pushing me away, disgust on her face.

Mom is forced to take time off work to buy me the jersey on credit at Meikles. I never tell her about the ear twist—only that I have been told not to return until I have the full school uniform.

Mom is my soft place to fall when things don't go well. She admits that she, too, had once faked illness as a child.

"I am glad you're not faking something today, but still went to school knowing you might get into trouble. It's better to be honest than say you're sick when you're not." She sighed. "You must get it from me," she said, as we shop for a school-approved jersey in Meikles. "It's probably in our genes. But I didn't think of doing that right away. It only occurred to me after something happened when I was about your age."

I want to hear her story. What is getting into our jeans? It's a visual I can't quite wrap my head around. Mom's childhood memories are vivid and fascinating, and I am awed at all the things she got up to. She was far worse than me! *She must have been just like one of the Bash Street Kids from Beano*, I think. "I hadn't prepared for a test," she tells me, as she picks up a blue jersey with my school colors, shaking her head as she examines the price tag. "Science was a subject I hated, so I dragged my feet walking to school."

I nod. I can definitely relate to this. We take the jersey over to the saleslady who looks askance at me, probably wondering why I am not in school.

"Put this on my account," Mom says. I shuffle my feet impatiently, but Mom waits, then, removing the price tag, she says, "Put it on."

The saleslady nods, understanding dawning on her face as I remove my red jersey and put on the blue one. "Oh, yes, the school…they're very fussy about uniforms. I get people in here all the time…" I don't care. I want to hear Mom's story. Finally, we're walking away, and Mom resumes.

"Where was I? Oh, yes, I was having a test and didn't want to get to school on time. I thought if I was late, I'd miss the test. On the way to school I went into the sweet store and bought some red sweets—a penny for six. They tasted like cinnamon. I sucked on one of them all the way to school, hoping I'd be late for the test, and I wouldn't have to do it."

I snort. "Did you get out of it?" I want to know if this strategy might be useful to me in the future.

Mom shakes her head. "Unfortunately, one of the teachers accosted me in the hallway, asking me why I was late. 'I'm sick,' I responded.

'Stick out your tongue,' the teacher said. So, I did. I stuck my tongue out, and the teacher screeched, 'This girl has scarlet fever! Get out of here, go home, *now*!'" Mom begins to laugh, one of her donkey brays. "My tongue was scarlet from the sweet I'd just eaten."

I laugh too until my eyes tear up. I wish it had been me who'd thought of this, although Mom insists it had all been accidental, and she'd been quickly cleared to return to school and do the test anyway. "I didn't try that again. You can't fool Ouma, either. She would have taken out a stick if I'd tried that again!"

It isn't only Miss Nettles I don't like, but she is the only teacher at this school who inspires profound terror in me and my peers. There are teachers with sharp stings in their voices, frowny faces, and an irritable impatience with slowness, but who do not cause truancy in me. One of them is Miss Thorne.

CHAPTER 23

READING MATTERS

Miss Thorne is a milder version of Miss Nettles. Unlike Miss Nettles, though, she is not sadistic. She has red hair and a short fuse. I find her somewhat intimidating, but she never terrifies me. She is my reading class teacher, and at age nine, during my first class with her, she gives us a reading test.

This test of progressively tricky words determines the reading level of each student. We are separated into groups according to the results. Each student is called up to the front of the class. Miss Thorne sits at her desk with the test— several sheets filled with increasingly difficult words—in front of her. We are allowed to make three mistakes before she stops us, and the place where we stop is our reading grade or level. When it comes to my turn, I begin to read as she points to each word. I notice the words become longer, containing more syllables, but it doesn't faze me. I read adult books. I am now reading a purloined copy of *The Diary of Anaïs Nin*. Mom would be horrified to know where her missing copy is—under my mattress. Anaïs Nin is a wonderful writer, I think, but it is full of unpronounceable French names and there are parts that are mystifying to me. By comparison, this test is easy. I continue to enunciate each word clearly and correctly. Out of the corner of my eye, I notice Miss Thorne's eyes swiveling toward me, her mouth slightly open. I continue reading through until we reach the end of the test. I have not made a single mistake.

"Wait here; don't move," Miss Thorne says in an uncharacteristically quiet voice. She rises and almost runs out of the room. I stand there, feeling as if I have done something terribly wrong. Or perhaps Miss Thorne has taken ill suddenly? The other students goggle at me, some with knowing smiles, others like Nikki, wide-eyed. Pie is in trouble! I begin to tremble. It feels as if I have stood there for hours, but it must only be minutes before Miss Thorne returns with a puzzled Mr. Winston in tow.

"I want you to listen to this," Miss Thorne says to Mr. Winston, and she indicates I should start reading from the beginning. I read again to the end of the test, with the same results as before. "What should I do with her?" Miss Thorne asks.

"Anything you like," Mr. Winston says, and leaves, giving me an inscrutable look on his way out the door.

While the rest of the class sits in groups reading, I sit by myself. I read Dickens, Homer, Poe, Dumas, Kingsley, and Baroness Orczy. I also enjoy the lighter children's books, mostly written by Enid Blyton. I devour books and am given free rein by Miss Thorne to read anything I like, as Mr. Winston has instructed. Mom has also given up trying to keep my reading matter restricted to appropriate books. She sometimes allows me to read her adult literature, books she recommends, such as those by Somerset Maugham. I read *The Moon and Sixpence*. Mom and I discuss the books we both read, and she always passes a good book on to me. We don't discuss Anais Nin, though. I return it back to Mom's library, half read, and she is none the wiser that it was ever missing.

Tea, Scones, and Malaria

CHAPTER 24

CHURCH

Mr. Brimstone grasps the raised pulpit of our small church, his finger stabbing skyward as he drones on. A sallow toothpick, his wrinkled face long frozen into a permanent expression of self-righteous anger and judgment, his voice trembles with satisfaction. He wags his finger. "…And He smote those who were wicked in the sight of the Lord…"

Forgetting for the moment where I am, I giggle out loud. An ominous hush falls over the congregation as heads swivel in my direction. Butch nudges me, and I look up from the *Beano* that I have hidden in my hymnbook. Mr. Brimstone's finger still points upward, his raisin eyes locking onto me, mouth half-open. A beat passes, then two, and I slowly fold up the comic book. I sit with my hands clasped on my lap, my eyes focusing on the puce curtains of the baptismal font behind Mr. Brimstone. Mom, sitting at the organ, shakes her head, lips compressed. I know by the look, the slight spark in her eye, that she will ask me for the *Beano* as soon as we get home.

Not to throw it away, but to read it herself.

Mr. Brimstone, satisfied I am no longer distracted, resumes his sermon. I wonder about the *smiting*, though. I've heard it often from Mr. Brimstone. The Old Testament God sounds like a psycho, one who roasts people alive and sends

143

terrible plagues to wipe out millions. Heaven does not sound so wonderful, either. It must be filled with people like Ouma and Mr. Brimstone. Those who are unlucky enough to make it there play harps all day. I don't think I'd like that. I can't even play the piano. Do they even have *Beanos* up there? But what other option do I have? Burning in hell is even worse than a Nuanetsi summer, Mom has told me, and it will go on forever and ever.

Our religion shall not be named, but something about it, perhaps the burnings, doesn't sit well with me. It gives me nightmares. I once stepped on a lump of live coal with my bare foot, so I know from first-hand experience how painful a burn can be.

During the sermons, I also distract myself with comic sketches in my little notebook of congregation members. They are not always complimentary. Correction—they are never complimentary. Sometimes the caricatures sit on clouds playing harps. My friends and I sit together as I sketch, trying unsuccessfully to smother our laughter. On occasion, we'll slip out when no one is looking and head for the corner store with our tithe money.

In our government school, religious classes are encouraged. Since our church is not represented, I am placed in the Catholic class. Our teacher, Mrs. Doolan, is obsessed with the Catholic saints. Every day she relates, with great relish, a story about a saint who has been burned, stoned, or otherwise tortured to death in horrible ways. Although they would hate to hear this, I think Catholicism has a lot in common with my family's religion—our fixation with death and dying.

Every week a running battle with Mom ensues. Our church day is Petina's day off, and Mom must get us dressed, fed, and shoehorn us into the car, all things she does not particularly relish. One week, the battle is especially arduous. We don't want to go. We loiter, linger, and complain. It is always the same refrain.

Mom: "Aren't you ready yet? Have you brushed your teeth?"

Us: "Why do we need to go? I have homework to do. Can't I stay home and do that, instead?"

Mom knows that it is only a ruse. As soon as she makes the mistake of leaving us at home, we'll be outside, playing.

Finally, with a sigh of relief, she sinks into the driver's seat after getting us into the car. The tires spit gravel as we peel out of the driveway; we are already late. Since Mom plays the church organ, there is a lot of pressure to get there on time. She pulls up into the last available parking spot in front of the little church, and we tumble out of the car. People are already walking inside. Mom notices, mixed with the smiles and nods, some strange looks directed her way. As she makes her way up the aisle to the organ in the front, something makes her glance down.

She is still wearing her fluffy pink bedroom slippers.

Tea, Scones, and Malaria

CHAPTER 25

MY TRIBE

In Africa, it is not only native Africans who are tribal. It is no different for us makiwas. White Africans, due to our sparse numbers, tend to form tribes, clans, who identify with each other for many reasons. We stick together like family. My tribe are all church members, unrelated close friends, and we all affect each other's lives in some way. In this part of the world, it is customary to call any family friend an "auntie" or an "uncle." Their children call my parents auntie and uncle, too. Like family, the tribe can be annoying, frustrating, loving, and intolerable all at the same time.

Some of the tribe are farmers. Auntie Sadie and Uncle Ruben Robinson, Auntie Lotte and Uncle Lars Hansen, and Auntie Claudia and Uncle Teo Ferreira —all live on nearby farms. Auntie Millie and Uncle Harry Hyde live on an asbestos mine, where Uncle Harry is a mineworker. Auntie Esme and Uncle Felix Willis are neighbors,

Most of these are the walking wounded, the damaged, the bruised psyches that cry out for help from the deaf and blind. It is the early Sixties, though, and any dysfunction is ignored, glossed over, or whispered about behind closed doors.

By contrast, Uncle Verne and Auntie Lenora—church members and business owners—appear quite normal. Their daughter is Georgia, a tomboyish girl who I think is a lot of fun. We children spend many weekends and vacations with these families, who all, except for Auntie Millie and Auntie Esme, have children our age or close to our age.

All these friends' children are more like an extended family to us. We grow up with them, and we stay in contact for the remainder of our lives. We fight, argue, play, and cry with them. We spend many weekends and holidays together and are often inseparable. While none of us are blood-related, there is no difference. We are family.

CHAPTER 26

THE ROBINSONS

Axel Robinson, the eldest child of the Robinsons, is my age—an overweight, pimply boy with a head like a shotgun slug. Ellie-May is a blonde doll of a girl the same age as Butch, and Freddie the same age as Queenie. Auntie Sadie, a sturdy-framed woman with a friendly, open face and black-currant eyes that sparkle with good humor, is one of the kindest people I've ever met. She possesses a passionate love for all animals. The Robinson's farmyard teems with cats, dogs, turkeys, ducks, and donkeys. If there is a heaven, I think, it must be Auntie Sadie's farm. I am obsessed with horses, and so is Auntie Sadie. Every Tuesday afternoon she picks me up after school and takes me to their farm to ride. Strangely, I've never fallen ill on a Tuesday. That is the healthiest day of the week for me.

Ruben Robinson, her husband, is bedeviled with a nature that bears little resemblance to his wife's. A squat man with close-cropped hair over a rugged, beefy face, he reminds me of a troll. While his wife is chatty with a ready laugh, Uncle Ruben glowers at us from under a battered, oil-stained fedora, as if he expects someone to come at him with the cattle-prod he uses quite readily on his kids. We keep a wary eye on him, and more than once I witness him cackling like a hyena as he chases his terrified, screaming children around the farmhouse with the prod. He is not above using it when he catches up with them. Auntie Sadie cowers in her bedroom during these events, and I often hear her sobbing. I think he has been at her, too, behind closed doors.

He never threatens his children's friends with the prod, but it scares us, and we feel helpless and heavyhearted for this sorry man and his family. His behavior indicates some deep, unhealed, festering wound that turns outward for relief. Other than that, he is a hard-working man, rising at dawn to work on his farm and only returning home at the set of sun. On rare occasions, I see him laugh, a glimmer of humanity that seeps from his soul, but it is unusual. His general demeanor explains a lot about his son, Axel, a bully, just like his father. He has learned well. I am often the target of Axel's bullying: donkey bites (a cupped hand slap), arm twisting, and other malicious behavior that is never corrected by an adult.

One Sunday, the farmyard is filled with vehicles parked alongside the driveway. People have arrived for Sunday dinner at the farm, and all the adults are indoors while the children play outside. Axel notices me inspecting two bicycles propped up against the verandah wall. He nods to his bike, a shiny red Raleigh with a high frame and downward curving handlebars.

"Do you want to learn how to ride? I'll teach you."

I nod eagerly. It is a strange offer for Axel, but I am not given to clarity of thought at age ten. Axel is not a generous kid, and he guards his bike as if it were a Ferrari. The smirk on his face should be my warning, but I want to learn how to ride a bike. It couldn't be more difficult than riding a horse, I think. He holds it for me while I clamber on, using the verandah steps to hoist myself up to the high saddle. Still grinning, but holding on, he pushes me toward the driveway as my feet flail desperately for pedals that I can't reach. A sense of panic and foreboding rises in my chest as Axel, chuckling, runs alongside me. It is when we get to the middle of the road that, with a final shove, he lets go of the bike, and I find myself careening down the driveway.

I grip the handlebars tightly, but I can't stop the bike.

"Where are the brakes?" I scream, but all I can hear is Axel's braying laughter behind me. *Are they those little levers that stick out just beyond the handlebars?* I am too afraid to unclench my death grip on the handlebars to try them. I want to jump off, but the ground is a long way down. The bike weaves drunkenly across the driveway heading toward the parked cars. I jerk the handlebars, and the bike lurches to the other side, barely missing another vehicle. To my horror, I am now teetering downhill toward more cars, and the bike isn't slowing. It speeds like a wobbly arrow down the driveway, aimed at none other than Mom's car. I must jump off, but I can't get my leg over the center bar. I am an unguided missile. I scarcely hear Axel's cackling as the scene begins to unfold in slow motion. With a tremendous crash and screech of metal, the bike hits Mom's Consul and topples, its front fender screeching down the side door. I tumble off, skidding on my hands and knees onto the gravely surface.

I rise and dust myself off. Ignoring Axel, who is inspecting his precious bike for scrapes, I take a deep breath. "I can ride a bike!" I yell through my tears to no one in particular. I can hear Butch calling for Mom from the front of the verandah.

"Pie just hit your car with Axel's bike," she yells.

What a little tattletale. I am still inspecting myself for damage, but I only have a scraped knee. Axel gets on his bike, making himself scarce as Mom emerges from the house, frowning. Walking down the driveway, I can see she isn't interested in my condition. Her eyes are fixed on the Consul. "What happened?" she asks, giving her car the once-over where the bike had hit it. "Not too bad," she says, shaking her head, then looking toward me as if she suddenly realizes I am part of the landscape. "Are you hurt?"

I lift my skirt. My knee is a bloody mess, but I am used to that. I skin them at least once a week. Mom takes me inside and washes off the blood. Ellie-May kindly offers me her bicycle to complete my bike riding lesson, and that day, I learn how to ride. The Consul is so beat up already that Mom says no one will notice a few more scrapes on its door. By no-one, she means Dad.

I take it all stoically and even become accustomed to Axel's bullying. It doesn't stop me from doing everything I can to spend a weekend on the farm. My love of horses and riding outweighs my apprehension of Axel. Ellie-May fears her brother as much as I do. She is as much a victim of his reign of terror as anyone else. He peeps through the keyhole at Ellie-May and me when we are in the bathroom. We tell Auntie Sadie, but she only grins and shrugs. "Boys! You can't change them."

CHAPTER 27

THE HANSENS

While Lotte Hansen seems normal, it doesn't take long for me to discover she is a religious fanatic who wants to control everything and everyone. A statuesque woman with a leathery face and booming voice, she tolerates very little from other church members that appears, in her eyes, "sinful." Her generous bosoms, like the cowcatcher on a locomotive, lead the way as she plows her way through life. Dad calls her his "bosom buddy," and he doesn't mean it positively. Lotte and her husband, Lars Hansen, are initially from Holland. I rarely see Uncle Lars. He spends most of his time outdoors, taking care of his dairy cattle, and only returning home for dinner. A jolly man with a sunburned face and a ready laugh, his Dutch accent is strong, whereas Auntie Lotte reveals only a small trace of an accent. One would think she had been born in England, but the Dutch décor in her house disabuses me of this notion.

Their daughter, Sophie, is a good friend. She is fiercely independent and speaks fluent Shona. On the weekends, when I am invited, we rise early in the morning to head out, barefoot, onto the farm. We enjoy plundering the guava and kumquat fruit trees growing around the house. Never bothering to wash anything first, we pop them into our mouth straight from the tree. We sample cattle feed directly from the bin or jump into the giant pit where it is stored to nibble on the brown, molasses-soaked ears of corn. For some reason,

153

we find the aromatic, sweetish corn-mix tasty. The cows thrive on it, growing fat and producing creamy milk. I am uncertain what it does for us, though. I remain as skinny as a starved rat.

Like those at Ouma's house or my great-grandfather's farm, evenings are spent in the living room, praying and reading the Bible. Uncle Lars sits in his overstuffed chair, the only comfortable piece of furniture in the austere home, puffing on his pipe. His expression remains a mix of tolerance and impatience. He accepts his wife's sincere devotion to her religion but steadfastly refuses to become a church member. Somehow, they remain married.

One day when I am around twelve, Butch and I, and Sophie, who is staying at our home for the day, decide to play dress-up. We get into Mom's makeup, perfume, and clothing. We can do that since she is at work. We are enjoying ourselves so much we don't hear Auntie Lotte's car pulling into the driveway or the front door opening. In Rhodesia, no one ever knocks; visitors walk in, and sometimes they may also ask what's for dinner. But Auntie Lotte isn't here for dinner. It isn't until I feel a firm hand on my neck and turn to face a wrathful Auntie Lotte that I realize we've been busted.

"What is that on your face?" she honks, her Dutch accent more pronounced than usual. Her nose twitches like an African hunting dog that has caught the scent. It is Mom's favorite perfume that I have liberally sprinkled over myself. "You stink! Are you little heathens? Get into the bathroom immediately and wash it off!" One by one, she pulls us into the bathroom and scrubs off Mom's lipstick, eyeshadow, perfume, and mascara with a rough washcloth. We try to explain we are only dressing up, but she isn't placated. "Dressing up like ungodly women, you are!" she roars as she soaps our faces. "Teaching my Sophie bad things!" She goes on in that vein until she ensures not a trace of the offending makeup is left on our glowing, burning skins. It is also not the last time in my life I will be referred to as a "little heathen."

Auntie Lotte takes over from Mom as the church organist. I think Mom is over-committed since she also teaches Sunday School. We groan to see Auntie Lotte sitting behind the old organ as we trudge into the church. Mom plays as if she is her favorite jazz artist, Charlie Kunz, with an upbeat tempo that has everyone smiling as they sing, but Auntie Lotte's pounding of the keys is wooden and ponderous, each note dropping on the ear like a lead ingot.

"I walked past your church last Sunday," says Nicki, my best friend who goes to the Greek Orthodox church. "I heard you all singing. Was it a funeral?"

"The whole town talks about your singing," says another friend. "Why can't you speed it up a little?"

I thank God they haven't heard Mr. Brimstone preach. He is the only church member that Auntie Lotte never criticizes. She may also be the only person who doesn't nod off during his sermons.

While Auntie Lotte is not my favorite tribe member, I am blessed with an extended family who is not so straightlaced. They are the Ferreiras.

Tea, Scones, and Malaria

CHAPTER 28

THE FERREIRAS

Auntie Claudia and Uncle Teo are close family friends who own a crop farm on the banks of the Lundi River. Auntie Claudia's ethereal beauty, chiseled features, and vibrant personality seem incongruous with the farm life she leads. I always feel she would do better in a city. She is a person who should be visiting the opera, frequenting art museums, and entertaining the rich and famous with teas and sundowners on a big lawn under a tent. She surrounds herself with bright colors, showing a flair for decorating and an eye for beauty. We spend many a happy weekend or holiday on this farm with their four girls, Rosa, Paloma, Livia, and Ida. Rosa is closer to my age, while Paloma and Butch are friends.

A cropped cut of brown hair tops uncle Teo's muscular build, full face, and piercing blue eyes. Teo's interests lie in farming. While he is a humorous and intelligent man, he does not possess the same passions as his wife. She loves to spend money. He is practical. She loves to entertain, but Teo is quieter, more at home with a cup of tea than buckets of champagne and revelry.

Mom is not impressed with Auntie Claudia. "She's flashy. Champagne tastes with a beer-bottle pocket," she sniffs one day in our presence, "and she also drinks way too much." With all the honesty that only a child can muster, Butch immediately relays this snippet of gossip to Auntie Claudia the next time we visit. The iciness between Mom and Auntie Claudia doesn't last long, though, and after a few months of not speaking, they resume their friendship. Mom had once dated Uncle Teo many years ago before she met and married Dad. Dad thinks she may still have some feelings for Uncle Teo. Mom assures him she doesn't. I also wonder if they had married, would I have been born? I ask Mom if I would have been a different person altogether or how much different my life would have been. Mom replies that it is an unanswerable question.

The Ferreira farmhouse is built of stone, with a breezy, screened-in verandah. The living room's dark blue walls and colorful furniture lends a festive air to the house. The kitchen is modern with wall cabinets—something I am not used to— and a fully stocked pantry. Auntie Claudia likes to shepherd us girls into the kitchen to bake something. I am always willing since I love to bake, but Butch and Rosa never stop complaining. They want to be outside, playing, and why isn't Rabbit included in this bake-a-thon?

"It's because he's a boy," says Butch, pouting as she measures the flour. There is more flour on her face and on the floor than in the bowl, I think.

"Dad wants to take us to see the cattle today!" Rosa is gritting her teeth as she cuts the butter into the bowl. "I don't want to make a stupid cake. Mom makes us do it because she's too lazy to bake."

"You'll find time to eat the cake, though," says Auntie Claudia, as she comes into the kitchen behind us. "You can still go with Dad. There's still plenty of time to make the cake. And sweep up the floor before you go."

After we've put the cake into the oven, we do get to go with Uncle Teo to inspect the cattle. He takes the bakkie, us kids sitting in the back of the small pickup truck as we bounce over rutted farm roads until we reach the cow pasture. We jump off the bakkie and run through the cattle herd picking out our favorite cows. They are dairy herds, and some of the cows have names. Uncle Teo lifts each of us to sit on the bony back of a Daisy or an Ella or a Mavis. The cows direct perplexed looks at us as they chew their cud and stubbornly refuse my pleas to gallop over the field. I want to ride them like horses, but they merely lower their heads and leisurely take another bite of grass.

The Ferreira's enjoy their booze perhaps a bit too much. Mom's observation is spot-on. Uncle Teo has built a still in the garage, or perhaps it is a brewery, where they brew homemade beer. They teach us kids to fill bottles with the brew when it is ready. At first, it seems like a harmless pursuit, even though we know our church does not approve of alcohol.

"Don't drink any, and most importantly, don't tell anyone about the beer brewing," Auntie Claudia admonishes us, with a pointed look directed at Butch. "You know how the church feels about alcohol." I agree with her. Anything I can do to rebel against the church is okay in my book.

We sip the brew when no one is looking, though, and although filling bottles could be a chore, we don't perceive it as such. The beer smells are heavenly, and the alcohol content is low enough so we don't get tipsy. But it soon becomes evident that the Ferreira's drinking does not stop at beer. Often, when we visit Auntie Claudia, she is overly bright in demeanor and her breath when she greets us with a hug smells of toothpaste or mouthwash. Mom gives Dad a knowing look.

"You don't brush your teeth in the middle of the morning," she says, later, on our way home. "I could smell the whiskey right through the Colgate."

Dad shakes his head, but again, no one says anything.

Shortly after we arrive in Fort Vic, when I am ten years old, Auntie Claudia procures three difficult-to-get tickets to a Peter Nero concert at the Civic Center. She and Mom agree that Auntie Claudia will take Rosa and me to the show. They both want us to cultivate a sense of culture, to familiarize ourselves with talent. Rosa and I are not so enthusiastic, but what choice do we have?

Peter Nero's career as a piano virtuoso has just begun to bloom in America, and here he is, visiting our backwater town. No one famous has ever visited Fort Vic, and even if he is, at this time, only slightly renowned, it is still an honor.

We dress up in our best church clothes, arriving early at the Civic Center. Auntie Claudia is wearing pearls and stiletto heels and trails a whiff of expensive perfume. We find our seats and settle down to wait. The auditorium is already full. A buzz of anticipation as the lights lower precedes the rise of the curtain. The audience claps decorously as the virtuoso enters. Mr. Nero strides confidently to the Steinway that stands alone on the stage, and with little preliminary, he sits and begins to play. *Haydn's Piano Concerto in D Major* swells and ripples through the air. The audience sits spellbound as I search for something interesting to look at in the auditorium. I examine the ladies' hairstyles in the row in front of us. I count the rows, squirming in my seat to see how many are behind us. I gaze upward at the ceiling—nothing compelling there—and then at my feet. I wish I had brought a *Beano* with me. Or my sketchbook…a book…any book. Rosa, a faraway look in her brown eyes, chews her fingernails to the quick, earning a slap from Auntie Claudia. We look at each other and sigh. A final crash of the keys indicates this piece has finally come to an end.

Good. Perhaps now it is over, and we can leave?

The audience roars. I clap enthusiastically, as does Rosa. We are both as thrilled to get to the end of this concert as I feel sure the pianist probably is. He rises and bows, but as if encouraged by the clapping and cheering, he sits down again, and my heart sinks as his fingers hover over the keys. As if not even slightly tired out by now, he plays one lengthy classical overture or piece after another.

"Gershwin's *Rhapsody in Blue*," whispers Auntie Claudia to her two catatonic charges. "You know, he'll only play on a Steinway!"

Like we care. We look at each other, rolling our eyes. My bottom hurts, and I shift uncomfortably in my chair, earning a glare from Auntie Claudia. It seems hours and hours have passed. Perhaps days. I stare at Auntie Claudia. The look of rapture on her face tells me she doesn't share our boredom. The pianist must have hypnotized everyone except Rosa and me. Every time Mr. Nero reaches the end of a piece, he stands up and bows to the audience. I sigh with relief. *It is over! We can go!* To my dismay, the audience rises to their feet, clapping more indecorously now, and shouting "Encore! Encore"

"What does that mean?" I ask Rosa. She shrugs. We soon find out. Mr. Nero sits and begins to play again. Each time we think it must surely be over, the audience yells, "Encore!" and it starts all over again. I grow to hate the audience. Finally, Mr. Nero gets tired, mopping his brow. Despite more shouts to continue from the audience, he takes a final bow and leaves.

Even though the concert backfires on her, Auntie Claudia has planted a slow-growing seed, a love of classical music in my psyche that takes years to mature. She does know what she is doing.

CHAPTER 29

THE HYDES

Another of the walking wounded is Auntie Millie, a close friend of Mom's from her school days and my godmother. She's a gentle woman with warm brown eyes and a wide mouth that can break into an infectious grin at a moment's notice. She is not a physically beautiful woman like Auntie Claudia, but her inner soul shines with grace and humor. She and Mom recall their college days with bouts of knee-slapping laughter, and it doesn't take much to get the two of them howling and dabbing at their eyes.

Millie has married a miner. Harry Hyde has a thin face, sallow skin stretched tight over high cheekbones and a balding head with thinning hair. Bloodshot, wintry eyes dart around as if tracking flies. His personality constantly duels with itself—one moment he is a garrulous, likable man with a ready laugh, until he takes a drink. That is when he morphs into a malignant monster. Millie bears the scars of her Mr. Hyde.

Harry works at Gath Mine, an asbestos mine about twenty-five miles away. We often visit them and, on a Sunday afternoon, walk down long, asbestos-filled tunnels dug out of the rock, marveling at how the fibrous ore is extracted from the earth. Once again, we are lucky. We never get lung disease or suffer ill effects from these deadly walks. We collect samples of asbestos and play with them. I like the feel of the silky fibers, and it never once occurs to anyone it might be dangerous.

One night in 1960 there is a knock at our front door. Dad is out on the job, so it's only us kids and Mom in the house.

"Who could that be, at this time of the night!" Mom grumbles as she cautiously opens the door. Butch, Queenie, and Rabbit are already asleep, and it is only I who am still awake. "Go back to bed!"

I retreat but hover in the background, my eye on the front door. A sobbing Millie stands on the porch.

"What's wrong?" Mom asks as if she doesn't know. "I didn't know you were coming."

Millie lifts her tear-streaked face, and the porch light reveals eyes swollen and blackened. "It's Harry. I can't take it anymore. He is going to kill me this time. I found the car keys and jumped in and drove away. I didn't take anything. I didn't stop until I got here."

Mom ushers her in, telling me sternly, again, to get back into bed, but I can still hear them talking. Pressing my ear against the door is helpful. They talk nearly all night, only going to bed in the wee hours. Mom must get up and go to work the next day, and I must go to school, where I am even more numb-skulled than usual.

I've heard Mom telling Auntie Millie, over and over, not to go back, to divorce him, but Millie always returns to the fray. She has no faith in her ability to support herself. Uncle Harry is a provider, if nothing else. Millie returns to Harry the next day, and it won't be the last time this scenario is repeated.

Mom unwisely sends Butch and me to visit Auntie Millie when she and Uncle Harry live in Bulawayo. At that time, we are a few years older, but we see, first hand, what it is like to be Auntie Millie. One evening, Harry staggers home after work, reeking of whiskey. He has stopped at the local pub for "a few." He turns his wrath on his wife for an imagined slight, an innocent comment she makes that hits the alcohol-saturated distortion field surrounding him and twists her comment into an attack on his manhood. If the abuse toward his wife isn't enough to quench his inner torment, he rounds on Butch and me, too, spewing hate and invective.

Butch and I flee, taking shelter on the fire escape outside the kitchen door. We hold each other, cowed and terror-stricken, as we listen to the raging storm inside. When Uncle Harry finally collapses in his bed, we tiptoe inside after checking that the coast is clear.

"Do you want to watch *The Beverly Hillbillies*?" Aunt Millie asks, turning on the black and white TV set. "I'll make some popcorn." Her eyes are bright with unshed tears, a determined grin plastered on her face. We sit and watch TV as if nothing untoward has happened.

It is the last time I visit with my godparents, but I dread that something might happen to Mom and Dad and I will have to go and live with them. That's what godmothers are about, isn't it? It is the stuff of my nightmares.

Tea, Scones, and Malaria

CHAPTER 30

THE KNIGHTS

Amongst our friends and fellow church members, the most normal are Verne and Lenora Knight, and their daughter Georgia. They are not local farmers, though. They own a filling station a few miles out of town. The drive to their home is spectacular. The road south weaves through massive, granite kopjes that rise on either side like gray bald heads, msasa trees clinging to crevices. One kopje looks like an elephant, its smooth sides resembling ears and a trunk that plunges into a deep, green forest valley. A broken, humped back rises behind the colossal head.

The Knights have a swimming pool in their front yard, which is the main attraction. Behind the house is an African church that we attend when visiting on weekends. The hymns are sung in Shona, and, just like Sophie Hansen, Georgia is fluent. I stumble along, but my voice is lost in the harmonious African voices that need no musical instrument. They clap and stamp feet, and it is much livelier than our dolorous singing at the white church in town. No one here nods off during the sermon. The African preacher encourages participation from the congregation, and their enthusiastic shouts of "*Yebo!*" intersperse his address.

When I am twelve, Georgia's parents, Auntie Lenora and Uncle Verne, invite me to vacation with them at the beach. I jump at the opportunity. The crisp five-pound note Mom gives me for my spending money is the most money I've ever had. I sit in the car, looking at it, holding it in my hand, examining the lines and colors on the note. I wonder if I'll ever see so much money again.

It is a two-day trip to South Africa's south-east coast, near Durban, in Uncle Verne's Mercedes. I have never been in such a posh car before. It smells new and purrs down the road without a single rattle or squeak. I sit in the back seat with Georgia and we plan how we will spend our pocket money. At the first opportunity once we reach the sea shore, we each buy a "Hug-a-Bug," a black blow-up plastic critter with big eyes and arms that wrap around our wrists. We are told by the store clerk it is the current rage amongst kids. We walk down the beach proudly displaying this cheap toy firmly attached to our forearms. It is the first time I've ever bought anything so frivolous, and I am heady with excitement. I imagine that all the other kids on the beach are staring at me in envy. I love the feeling.

Georgia's grandparents live in a mansion on a hill that overlooks the blue Indian Ocean. Her grandfather is the mayor of the town, and now my dream of luxurious living is complete. Georgia and I have also split the cost of a "lilo," an inflatable mattress meant for the water. Since the house sits on a hill with a terraced lawn to the main road below, we use the plastic lilo as our sled. We start at the top terrace by the driveway and toboggan down seven grassy terraces, screaming as if we are on a carnival roller-coaster. Although Georgia's grandfather patches the lilo up for us repeatedly, it finally falls apart, turning into a limp, uncooperative sheet of plastic. We lose interest in the lilo and spend the rest of our money on ugly plastic dolls with pink hair that are called "trolls."

While swimming in the ocean, I feel a prick on the top of my foot. "Ouch!" I exclaim and promptly forget about it. A few hours later, my foot swells up, and waves of pain, excruciating pain, begin to envelop my foot. The area is red and inflamed, and Auntie Lenora gives me an aspirin and a band-aid. I spend several sleepless nights tossing and turning in pain before the foot returns to normal on its own. I never learn what my foot encountered in the ocean, but the agony it caused me is unforgettable.

Our farmer friends live well, but not like rich people. The Knights give me a brief glimpse of what it must be like to never worry about money.

Thanks to my prolonged exposure to these friends, my tribe, my earlier fears of makiwas gradually diminish. I no longer feel like a zebra on the savannah surrounded by hungry lions and crocodiles. Nightmares of Miss Nettles, Dr. Sykes, and black mambas slithering through my psyche fade. I am now part of a pride of lions, a pride who will keep the predators— people who torment me with foul language and rulers—at bay. The tormenters become fangless demons of the past, even objects of pity, and sometimes dark humor that manifests in my notebook: cartoon figures, balloons emerging from their mouths that say silly things. I laugh my nightmares away, and my friends join me in the ridicule.

Tea, Scones, and Malaria

CHAPTER 31

OUR NEW HOME

The house that Dad built in Fort Victoria.

1961 is the year I turn eleven, and it is the year Yuri Gagarin becomes the first man in space. While this is a momentous occasion, it can't compare to the completion of our new home that Dad has built. It isn't a house paid for and owned by the government, like the one at Buffalo Bend. It isn't a rental. It is ours, lock, stock, and barrel. Dad has built the house in his spare time on a land plot we've bought in a new suburb in the northern section of town. We are now suburbanites.

The house is ranch-style, an "H" shape with a flat concrete roof on the center section and peaked tin roofs on the side sections. We are explicitly warned never to climb up to the roof, but a nearby ladder ensures we climb up to the flat top as often as possible. We gingerly step between uncovered electrical lines to find a spot in the sun where we can survey the world.

Fronting the house on the other side of a broad dirt road, an empty expanse of savannah stretches to the horizon. Homes here are spaced far apart. We feel as if we are in the bush again, only now with electricity and running water — water we can drink straight from the tap, or garden hose, in our case.

Mom hires a gardener, and soon the front yard bursts forth with lawn, shrubbery, and colorful flower beds. Flowering vines cascade across the dark beams of the pergola Dad built next to the house.

Behind Petina's quarters is a utility lane meant for the "jam truck," a sewage tanker that comes once a week and pumps out our septic tank. The aroma heralds the jam truck's approach long before it reaches our property. On the other side of the utility lane are vacant plots that afford us a vast playground. On one of these plots, a tree of some kind grows: smooth-barked, it spreads out healthy, twisty branches that crisscross over each other. This tree becomes our ship, plane, house, or whatever we want it to be. We parachute out of the plane by jumping off one of the lower branches. We clamber to the ship's crow's nest to look for icebergs. We each have our own "home" in different parts of the tree. We spend hours in this tree, and it is a favored hangout for us and the neighborhood children.

Our preferred pastime, though, is to wander the bush in front of the house. In the rainy season, we splash through puddles of water, looking for the edible wild grape. This vine grows close to the ground and produces juicy clusters of purple grape-like fruit. Flame lilies bloom at this time of year, and we pick them to take home to Mom. The flame lily is Rhodesia's national flower. We look for red velvet mites, tiny spider-like creatures that look like scarlet pincushions with legs, and we let them run over our hands. This is the only spider I have never been afraid of. They are much too pretty to inspire fear in me.

In the dry winter months, we gather the tops of the tall elephant grass together to form tents, or 'forts.' We search for the antlion, a fearsome but tiny creature with massive jaws that makes its home in dry, sandy areas. Its home is a trap for unwary ants or other small insects. Funnel-shaped, it traps anything small enough to fall into it. The antlion pounces, the ant disappearing into a pair of enormous mandibles. We tickle the funnel with a twig or grass stalk, just to see the creature leap out of its lair, jaws snapping. To us, it is a science-fiction monster inhabiting an alien planet.

Since we are now further out of town, we at first rely mostly on Mom chauffeuring us to school and wherever else we need to go. Mom finds that not only burdensome but inconvenient since she works full-time. They must pay for the house, and they want to ensure they have enough savings. We are coming out of the woods financially, and Mom and Dad decide they can now afford to buy us bicycles. My first bicycle is a Raleigh, a blue girl's bike that I ride to school or into town. I enjoy my new-found independence to come and go as I please.

We play with the neighborhood kids who also have bicycles, and we race up and down the dirt road in front of our house. That is how my knees are always skinned and grazed. I often get into the road's sandy verge, and my wheels skid off the road, depositing me ungracefully on the gravely surface. We never wear helmets or knee pads since they're unheard of at this time.

Another advantage of having our own transportation is that no one has to be in the car with Mom. Mom's car is a second-hand Consul from the 50s, but she drives it as if she is Sterling Moss in a Ferrari on the race track at Le Mans. Neighbors often notice her flying down the road surrounded by a cloud of dust.

"Like a bat out of hell," comments one of our neighbors to me as she stands in her front yard. "Who does she think she is, Roy Rogers?" The name sticks. Mom is proud of her moniker, and we soon learn that neighbors' comment, "Roy Rogers rides again," every time she drives past the houses on our street. Still, Mom is handy in taking us places where our bikes are not practical. Such as movies. Movies add a new facet to our lives here in Fort Victoria.

CHAPTER 32

OUR SMASH HIT

1962

Movies have become essential in our lives. Fort Victoria possesses a theater, but our school also shows movies on Saturday nights in the auditorium to the pupils and parents. Old black and white Movietone newsreels from years back, perhaps WW2, begin the evening. A warm-up before the main attraction. Sometimes, we have even older shorts, such as Laurel and Hardy, Charlie Chaplin, and the Marx Brothers, that leave us howling with laughter.

We are spell-bound. *Pollyanna* is one of my favorite movies. Butch is the spitting image of Haley Mills, who plays the leading role. I'll admit, I am jealous. Butch, despite her name, is a pretty girl with blonde hair, blue eyes, and an upturned nose. People can't get enough of her, and boys are beginning to notice her.

I am a skinny kid with spiky brown hair that looks as if it has been chewed by rats during the night. My knees are always grazed due to my dubious bike skills, and my gap-toothed smile graces many a school photo. I dream that one day I will be as beautiful and talented as Doris Day or Sophia Loren, and boys will notice me, too. Unfortunately, my crush,

Mario, the Italian boy in my class, will remain forever unaware of my existence.

Dad only goes to the movies with us if there's a John Wayne movie showing, but we don't care. We will watch anything. Mom feels the same way. Even an old Charlie Chaplin movie has us piling into the car as if it is a hit debut. For us, it *is* a debut, no matter how old. Mom's favorite movies are *Gone with the Wind* and *The Wizard of Oz*. She says they take her back to her childhood when movies were her escape from reality. They still are. She has been smitten with Clark Gable for eons, but to me, he is a creepy old man with a creepy little mustache. I can't figure out what she sees in him.

Inspired by our weekly movie addiction, we decide we're going to make our own movie. Mom acquires a Bell & Howell 8mm movie camera and is eager to begin her first excursion into cinematography. We scout out a location, exploring the bush's expanse in front of our house. We decide unanimously on the Shagashe River, where the railway bridge spans its shallow, rocky width. For our production of *Moses in the Bulrushes*, this is the perfect spot. It has all the elements, including bulrushes. The movie is now in pre-production mode, and that takes—well, not more than ten or fifteen minutes. What takes much more time is the endless fighting. Who will be the star of this show? Who will be delegated to the lesser roles? We argue endlessly about who will wear what costume. The chief complainer, of course, is me. Why can't I wear Butch's costume and why must I wear Dad's bathrobe? Accusations of unfairness and favoritism fly.

The producer, Mom, is pulling her hair out in chunks before filming has even begun.

"I've produced plays in the past," she tells us. "Before I married your father, I produced and starred in a stage production of *Little Women* for our church." She directs a glare at us that could ignite a bush fire. "Never have I ever come across such silliness. If you don't like your role or costume," she points to the door, "leave. You don't have to be a part of this. Your roles are all important. Now shut up and let's get on with it."

The starring role is an unsurprising choice. It is established quickly after Mom's ultimatum, most unfairly, in my opinion. Butch will have the leading role, that of the Egyptian princess. Despite my dreams of being on a par with Sophia Loren one day, the producer is right. I am not princess material, so Miriam's role is unquestionably mine. Dad's striped terrycloth bathrobe is also mine to wear. With a towel around my head, I am now an Israelite slave girl.

Filming begins the weekend after the purchase of the camera. There will be no problem with gawking spectators. The railway bridge and surrounding area are far from the beaten paths of curious onlookers. That is fortunate. Any passerby who happens to catch a glimpse of the crew and cast will be baffled and maybe even concerned by our strange attire.

A sleepy lizard sunning itself on a rock is the only witness to this memorable day in cinematic history. We file our way down a narrow path toward the river bank. The lizard opens one eye and decides it does not want to be a part of whatever is happening and scuttles into the bushes.

Rabbit, from the beginning, has been shanghaied unwillingly into this movie. He has no interest in the performing arts. He makes that plain by wearing a scowl throughout the filming. He is a bare-chested soldier in the entire Egyptian army's composite role with a towel wrapped around his waist and tied in place with a string. He carries a stick we have found near the river bank—his spear. His role is not a speaking one (none of us have a speaking role since the camera does not have sound). Still, it is an important role. He must brandish the stick frequently and aggressively at critical points in the movie when instructed to do so by Mom and scowl even more than usual. He, too, is perfect for the role.

Queenie is more problematic. She is too old to be Baby Moses and too young to be a significant character, so she becomes the obsequious slave girl. She is supposed to carry a palm frond to wave over the princess's blonde head as she makes her way down to the water's edge. We don't have palm trees in the bush, so the Prop Department substitutes the palm frond with a small branch of a nearby leafy bush. Queenie is eager to please, thrilled to be included in our production. She has been subjected in pre-production to many snarky comments by her fellow cast members regarding her acting abilities. She smiles happily throughout the shooting and waves the 'palm frond' a tad too energetically, but no-one wants to discourage her.

Wardrobe has made up the princess's costume using a collection of the stiff chiffon ballerina-type petticoats popular in the '60s. They stick out at an angle, many-colored, like a tutu. Her top is something sparkly with sequins that we discover in Mom's ragbag. A wreath of silvery Christmas tinsel shimmering in the bright sunlight sits on her head.

"Why should she have all the fun costumes?" I whine as I stare down at the drab bathrobe. Mom had nixed my demand to wear a tinsel crown, too.

Mom yells, "Action!" and "Stations!" She doesn't have a megaphone, so she uses her cupped hands through which to shout. None of us knows what "action" or "stations" means, but neither does Mom. She has seen this being done in movies, and it seems like the right thing to do. We continue to mill around, distracted by the Egyptian army poking a frog with his spear. Finally, the scene begins to unfold.

Furtively dramatic, I creep down to the water's edge carrying an old basket with the baby Moses, a plastic doll wrapped in a towel. The Egyptian army shows himself by waving his spear menacingly as I sneak from one bush to another. After much hissing from the producer to "get on with it," I easily outmaneuver the dim-witted army and finally reach the water. I place the basket containing baby Moses carefully in the river. It promptly sinks. I quickly retrieve baby Moses from his watery grave. He and the basket are filmed "floating" down the river, assisted by my hand, to a clump of bulrushes a few feet away.

It is now time for the princess to make her grand entrance, for which she has been patiently waiting. She sweeps majestically toward the water, tossing her long blonde hair over her shoulder as her tinsel crown glitters. Her adoring slave sweeps the branch back and forth over her head as if shooing a swarm of killer bees away. Upon reaching the water, the princess gives a startled, theatrical spasm as she pretends, for the first time, to catch sight of the basket—with my hand still attached. Pointing dramatically, she orders the slave girl to bring her the basket. She doesn't say anything, but the hand signal conveys the message very well. She is a natural.

Back home, we proudly review our handiwork on a white bedsheet stuck with tape to the wall as the projector whirrs through the small 8mm spool. We are no longer cast members and crew but now the uncritical audience. The camera pans the river in jerky motions, and here and there we catch glimpses of the railway trestle bridge in the background. We don't deem this much of a problem. We cheer and jeer as various characters silently appear and disappear, like an old Chaplin movie. It is our smash hit!

CHAPTER 33

PETINA AND JOHNNY M'BARRO

Petina adds a new member to our tribe: A son, Johnny M'Barro—Johnny Wheelbarrow—is born in 1962. She calls him by this name because she keeps him in a wheelbarrow outside while she works. Many African women keep their children on their backs, fastened securely with a cotton cloth length. Petina prefers the wheelbarrow, only fastening Johnny on her back when it is necessary.

The servant's quarters in the back yard consist of a small kitchen, a bathroom, and a bedroom. The first thing Petina does is place her bed up on bricks, raising it a foot higher from the floor. "For the tokoroshe," she explains. "He not see my face when I sleep." According to African belief, the tokoroshe is a little creature that preys on sleeping people. By raising her bed, he will not be able to gaze upon her as she sleeps, which is not a good thing. Since we live in town, the nganga is no longer a threat, so she threatens Queenie with the tokoroshe. Butch, Rabbit, and I are too old to be frightened by her boogiemen anymore. If Queenie refuses to eat her food, the tokoroshe will come and get her. Queenie learns about dinosaurs from us older kids, and Petina is quick to pick up on this new boogie man. The tokoroshe is consigned to the bin, while the "dinner-saur" becomes the new threat.

We like to gather around the communal pots with Petina in her quarters and whoever happens to be eating with her. Despite her eye disfigurement, she doesn't have any problem with male companionship, only marriage.

We prefer Petina's food over Mom's uninspiring mess of boiled meat and potatoes with a serving of rice and overcooked vegetables. We hang outside Petina's quarters in the back yard, drawn in by the aroma emanating from her kitchen. Sadza is the primary African staple, a cornmeal porridge cooked to a stiff consistency, served with aromatic meat, gravy, and greens. She teaches us how to eat in the traditional, African way: with our hands. She shows us how to squat on the floor around the communal pots, and, using our right hand, we scoop a small handful of sadza from the pot, squeeze it into a little ball, then dip it into the meat and gravy. I use my left hand, which I often do since I am still a southpaw despite Auntie Isabelle's best efforts. Petina sternly shakes her head and redirects me to use my other hand. In African tradition, the right hand is the "clean hand," while the left is only used for unclean tasks. The food tastes heavenly no matter which hand I use.

Since Mom rarely disciplines us, and Dad is absent most of the time, Petina takes on the role of drill sergeant. She never beats us—Africans abhor this practice, considering it barbaric. Instead, she yells a lot, shakes her finger in our faces, and threatens to tell Mom. Sometimes she does. Her most frequent complaint is the state of our bedrooms. We hate cleaning or tidying up, which does not sit well with Petina.

Petina ambushes Mom outside as she comes home from work.

"You will get into your bedrooms right now and I want to see them sparkle," Mom says as she walks into the house. She's irritated. She's had a long day, and she's already told us more than once to clean up. Petina stands behind her, shaking her head, glowering at us. I stick my tongue out when Mom isn't looking, and Petina makes a clucking sound.

I wonder if she'll tell Mom I haven't done my homework, either. She does. Mom threatens to tell Dad when he gets home. Dad is her ace in the hole. We scurry into our rooms and begin to clean up, but the next day, the rooms look as if they've been ransacked again by a barrel of marauding vervet monkeys. It is an ongoing battle, and one Petina always loses. Mom tells us that we are privileged to even have homework.

"Petina didn't have the opportunities you kids have," she says after we've admitted we haven't even cracked a book after coming home from school. "On the Reserves, where we found Petina, African girls need to rise early in the morning, before the sun comes up, do their chores, and then walk miles, barefoot, to a school—if they're lucky enough to have one. You kids don't know how lucky you are."

We are Petina's family. It is how we feel about her and how she feels about us. She considers Queenie a daughter for all the many years she remains with us since she has raised her from a baby. Queenie is just as devoted to Petina. Like Silas with Rabbit, Petina often protects Queenie from Dad's wrath. We resent this, and Queenie is all too aware of the situation. Mom and Dad are lax with discipline when it comes to their youngest. Butch, Rabbit, and I are at school when Queenie tries her hand at a crayon mural on one of the house's walls.

"Who did this?" Dad growls as he points to the artwork decorating the hallway walls. Petina hovers in the background, a faint expression of worry on her face. Can she protect her charge from this? The evidence is irrefutable, and as Queenie's defense lawyer, Petina must think quick, but five-year-old Queenie is quicker. Folding her arms, crayon still in hand, she announces with a straight face: "Butch did it."

Petina and Dad convulse with laughter, Petina slapping her hands together as Queenie glows with a lie well-told. Dad paints over the offending work, and Mom tells us when we come home how we were blamed for something we did not do. We take it well, we think.

CHAPTER 34

TEA AND CANNABIS

Dad's job once again takes him away to far-away places, several hours drive over rough roads. He remains at a site Monday through Friday and returns home for the weekends.

Dad has refurbished an antique Armstrong-Siddeley, a British car built in the 1930s or '40s. Gunmetal gray, it has a long nose with a V-shaped radiator grille. It was a prestigious car in its era, but now, like an old dowager turned bag-lady, it has seen better times. Dad bought it for a pittance since it had been up on blocks for many years. He spends every weekend at home restoring it, but unfortunately, never to its original splendor. Still, Dad is as proud of the old girl as a man can be. The floorboards have gaping holes, and every time he drives through a puddle, brown muddy water sprays up into the car, soaking the driver and passenger. He drives the Siddeley to his campsite and home again every Monday and Friday, and he is right; the old dame is nothing to look at, but thanks to his TLC she runs well.

Dad decides that it is a good idea for us kids to spend a week or two with him in the bush during the school holidays. We readily agree. Bush camping is fun for us, and it will give Mom and Petina a break. We eagerly pile into the Siddeley and set off for an area about fifty miles away where Dad is building yet another bridge. We love this river. I no longer remember which one it is, but it runs swift and strong over rocks and boulders, forming sheltered pools that are (perhaps) crocodile-free where we can swim. The local African kids also know these pools and frequent them as often as we do. We trust their opinion about the pool's safety and swim with them. We don't understand each other's language, but it doesn't seem to be a problem for anyone. Issues are resolved by some half-hearted splashing, insults hurled in English and Shona, but we are back to playing after a minute or two.

Every morning I wake up in my bed in the tin hut where we sleep to an odd smell in the air. It is not one of the familiar aromas of the bush. I wrinkle my nose, trying to place the woody, herbal odor, but it eludes me. We get dressed, eat a quick breakfast of toast or cereal, then disappear into the bush.

At dusk, we return to Dad's camp, often lured by the enticing aroma of *maboa*, termite mound mushrooms, fried in butter. In the rainy season, these meaty, earthy white mushrooms grow to enormous sizes. They remind me of the Big Ears character, a dwarf who lives in a toadstool home, in the *Noddy* books of Enid Blyton. I want to find a whopper of a mushroom so I, too, can hollow it out and live in it. Mostly, though, our dinner is bland rice, canned vegetables, and venison. We are tucked early into our beds in the tin shack, mosquito netting draped over our beds like a shroud, lulled to sleep by raindrops on the tin roof, a frog chorus, and the nightjar's "*good lord deliver us*" call.

Each evening the mysterious morning odor has disappeared, leaving no trace. It is only later, when we return home, that we hear Dad telling Mom how he caught his cook, Tendai, smoking cannabis, or *dagga,* in the local lingo.

"He smokes it outside every morning."

Mom glances at us, sitting nearby. "I don't like it. Not around the kids."

"Africans have a different attitude towards *dagga* than we do. It is a big part of their spiritual practices and Tendai says it gives him strength. If I had to fire every worker for using it, I wouldn't have anyone who would work for me."

Mystery solved, but I don't know what cannabis is, anyway. I think it must be some type of tobacco. I decide I don't like the smell.

It is here, at Dad's job site, that it becomes evident how much my parents love their tea. Dad has another worker besides Tendai, a young man whose only job is to make tea all day long. When Dad finishes a pot of tea, the man takes it back and returns quickly with a fresh pot. We drink loose leaf tea grown in the highlands of Kenya steeped in a teapot topped by a knitted or crocheted tea cozy to keep it warm. Dad likes his strong, while Mom likes hers weak with plenty of milk and lots of sugar. Dad scorns Mom's weak tea. "Her tea isn't weak, it's a fortnight," he always comments, so the tea man makes it to his specifications—a dark, reddish-brown concoction with a bitter tannin flavor.

Our relationship with our tea is much like that of the Japanese in their tea ceremony. We do not show disrespect toward our tea. Rhodesians also never use teabags. Teabags are floor sweepings for the uninitiated. That is a sacrilege. If you don't know how to brew tea properly using loose leaf tea in a pot, you aren't worthy of calling yourself a Rhodesian. I am taught how to make tea at age five and how to do it correctly. We also know how to pour and serve it the right way. Cream is not used with tea, only milk, and a small amount is poured into the teacup before adding the brew. Sugar, in lump form, is the accepted way to sweeten tea. Only, we can't afford lump sugar, which is more expensive, so our sugar bowl contains ordinary sugar that is lumpy from wet spoons.

Even in the bush, we manage a semblance of civility; tea is our ritual, a routine that borders on the spiritual. It is one indulgence that we can afford. It makes a harsh life more tolerable, and our tea-fetish is no different to Tendai's daily cannabis ritual. That's why Dad tolerates the cannabis. He understands.

CHAPTER 35

MALARIA

Mom and Dad both suffer recurring bouts of malaria every year. It manifests as chills and feverishness.

We are all supposed to take prophylactics, but since they are bitter, we illogically hold them in our mouths until Mom's back is turned, and then we spit the pill out. There are consequences, though. In 1963, when I am nearly thirteen and in my first year of high school, I get malaria. It begins with the chills and shakes, so Mom keeps me home from school and goes to work. As the day progresses, I feel worse. I run to the toilet to throw up: a black, dark vomit that looks like coffee grounds, and stagger back to bed. Usually, I enjoy a reprieve from school even through sickness, since any illness is better than Miss Nettles and others like her. Still, I am not enjoying my day off this time.

I fall asleep, and as I do so, I feel myself rising out of bed. To my great joy, I feel chipper—no nausea, headache, or sickness. I notice almost peripherally that the bed is still occupied by someone, a lump that lies motionless under the blankets. I feel myself rising and floating at the ceiling level out of the room and down the passage. I am preoccupied with the pattern Dad has made in different color tiles on the floor. I have never seen it from this height. At that moment, I hear a car pull up into the driveway, so I waft, light as a feather, back to my bed. A few minutes later, Mom walks into the bedroom. It feels as if I had been hit in the head with a two-by-four. I shiver and shake, and my teeth rattle. Mom places her hand on my head, then shouts for Dad, who is doing something outside — probably working on his car.

"This child is burning up!" she says to him as he walks in. "She's delirious."

I am insisting that our white terrier dog, Spooky, has just pushed me out of bed.

"What should I do?" Mom asks.

"Call the doctor."

So, Mom runs next door (we still don't have a phone) and calls the doctor, the same Dr. Sykes who had removed my appendix. When he arrives, he examines me briefly and pronounces, "She's faking it. There's nothing wrong with her." He rises and leaves. Mom is panicked, and even Dad looks worried. They both know I am not faking illness this time, but how can they treat me without medication? Somehow, I pull through this bout of malaria after a few days and return to school. I do keep getting recurrences, just like my parents, but it never kills me.

What is worse, though, is when Dad gets hepatitis, or "yellow jaundice," from contaminated food on the job. He brings it home to us. First Rabbit turns yellow, although he recovers pretty fast from the jaundice, then I get it. I am still weakened from my bout with malaria. I am confined to my bed for six weeks, unable to eat anything except fish, rice, and sugary stuff. I am okay with the sugary stuff, but I crave fatty foods. When someone—Butch—sneaks me a meat pie or something forbidden, I suffer for days after with nausea and vomiting.

I finally recover, but I am a yellow skeleton. I have missed a lot of school. In 1963 Martin Luther King gives his "I have a dream" speech in Washington, D.C. I have a dream, too— to do well in my schooling, but I am still recovering from my bout with malaria and hepatitis and must catch up on what I have missed.

Surprisingly, my first year turns out better than my other school years combined despite my prolonged absence. I have compassionate and caring teachers who encourage me to do well, especially in areas I do not excel in. At the year-end exams, my marks place me at the top of the class. My improved grades surprise me as much as my astonished parents, but I credit my teachers for that accomplishment. They care enough to encourage me in my weak areas and do not choose to belittle their students or make them afraid. My illnesses have not held me back.

Tea, Scones, and Malaria

CHAPTER 36

FOOD ADVENTURES

1963

Mom fancies herself a cook. We don't disabuse her of the notion. Sometimes she'll come up with something tasty, such as a sticky marula jam, scones, or jam tarts. She invests in a pressure cooker, but that is only the beginning of our kitchen disasters. I don't remember exactly how many times the pot explodes, its lid flying off like an unguided missile, contents ending up on the kitchen ceiling. Luckily none of us are ever hurt, but that is because no one really enjoys hanging about in the kitchen while the pressure cooker hisses and spits on the stove.

I will not forget Mom's birthday cakes with their sunken middles and sticky bottoms, the dense textures glued together with frosting. Mom tries her best, saying that her mom couldn't cook worth a damn, so she wants to be a better cook than Ouma. Unfortunately, her dream remains unrealized, but I understand. Ouma's uninspired boiled cabbage, potatoes, and meatballs will live long in infamy in our memories.

"Ouma was never interested in cooking," Mom says. "Oupa used to do all the cooking before he…" She can't finish. I know what she means, though. "I used to go into the kitchen and cook as a child," she continues, "but the maid complained too much about the mess I made. Ouma put a stop to my cooking attempts. I am getting better now, though, aren't I?"

I nod, crossing my fingers. When I am twelve, I begin to take an interest in baking, mostly out of self-preservation.

My interest in cooking has not escaped the notice of Auntie Esme, our Lebanese neighbor. She has a reputation for taking her cooking seriously. Her heavy-set frame is a testament to her kitchen skill. Low fat or healthy food is not her forte, and she uses lard liberally, which makes her food all the more delicious. She takes me under her wing, telling me to come over every day after school; she will teach me to cook. I love to go over there, but only when her husband isn't home.

She has married a man similar in nature and habit to Uncle Ruben and Uncle Harry. If one squished the two of those men together, as if squeezing putty figures into one mass, one would get Uncle Felix. Auntie Esme, like Aunt Millie, is often covered in bruises. She takes the beatings stoically, never complaining, but everyone knows what is going on. And no one ever does anything about it.

It is in her kitchen, though, where Auntie Esme rules. I don't think even Uncle Felix would dare to enter her domain, and it is a great honor to me to be invited in. She is an artist who takes pride in her skill and artistry, shunning all help from well-meaning dinner guests. She uses ingredients in her dishes unheard of in my home: garlic, olive oil, and fragrant spices.

"Now, remember what the names of these are," she tells me as she vigorously sprinkles the spices over a whole chicken, the batwing under her arms jiggling. "Write them down." I do that, then promptly lose the list. She makes me peel pomegranates, scooping out the messy seeds inside, so she can place them in the pot with the chicken, along with bunches of fresh parsley. "And you always save the fat," she says, scooping it up from the chicken broth after it has cooked. It's pure gold."

I love the smell of garlic. I realize now, to my relief, after having seen a Boris Karloff movie, that I can't possibly be a vampire. I want to string it up all over the house so that I'll be safe from vampires, but Mom never buys garlic.

We have invited Auntie Esme to my thirteenth birthday party, a small affair with a few friends. I have baked my birthday cake, free of Mom's supervision: a three-layer sponge, ordinary perhaps, but not burned on the edges or sunk in the middle. I have separated the layers with butter icing and carefully piped colorful decorative rosettes onto the top layer. I am given the honor of cutting the cake, and I place a generous slice on a plate for Auntie Esme. With an inscrutable expression, she lifts the plate, holding it up to eye-level. Wordlessly, she places it back onto the table, picks up her fork, and takes her first bite, chewing thoughtfully. She takes another bite, then another. I am unable to take my eyes off her. I don't hear what anyone is saying to me. My hands tremble. Finally, she finishes the slice of cake and lays her fork down. She raises her eyes, looking directly into my terrified face.

"Light. Airy. Tasty. You have done well. Congratulations."

For my birthday gift, Mom and Dad subscribe me to a *Cordon Bleu* correspondence course. Each month I receive a new lesson in the mail, a glossy, beautifully illustrated booklet that becomes part of a volume. It has step-by-step instructions, a glossary, and recipes. I learn how to make authentic Austrian strudel, *coq-au-vin*, and many other international dishes. I discover that cooking is an art in itself, and I challenge myself to create more complicated dishes. I am tired of our bland and humdrum fare: rice, meat, and potatoes. My strudel demands a table all to itself as I stretch the dough over the table until it is onion-skin-thin and then roll it up with the raisins and apples inside. It is delicious.

On our visits to our farmer friends, food is always at the center of our social interactions. We help churn butter made with cream from cows that have been milked that morning. We slather thick slices of home-made bread fresh from the oven with butter, drizzling it with honey. We wander the vegetable patches, eating vegetables straight from the field: sun-warmed, just-ripened tomatoes, snappy green beans, and juicy red strawberries plucked from thickly laden runners.

Sometimes when we visit Auntie Claudia, she ushers us, along with her four daughters, into their enormous farmhouse kitchen. "Today, we're making *koeksisters*," she orders. Auntie Claudia is very bossy, I think. She always keeps us busy doing something, and by "we," she means us girls. Rabbit will get off scot-free. "It's constructive, and a learning experience for you," she explains. We groan. We know it's also going to be a lot of work. Traditional *koeksisters*, pronounced "cook sisters," is an Afrikaner delight made of braided strips of pastry, deep-fried, drenched in syrup, and sprinkled with cinnamon. You can't eat just one, and sticky fingers are an indelible part of the experience.

Our family experiences a time of plenty during the early Sixties. Our farmer friends supply us with whatever we need. They arrive at the house, often just as we're sitting down to our evening dinner, laden with baskets of produce and fresh eggs. In our tribe, it is considered insulting not to invite guests to sit down and eat with you. Everyone knows this, so arriving a few minutes before dinner is often a strategic move. Mom rolls her eyes when she catches sight of a farm vehicle pulling up in the driveway.

"Oh no! The Robinsons are here. All of them. I can't complain, though," she says as she tells Petina to bring in more plates, and we scoot over at the table to make room for the unexpected guests. "They never arrive empty-handed."

We kids wander around in the bush during school vacations, foraging for whatever fruits we can find. Marulas, the favorite of elephants, is also our favorite. Mom makes a sticky, toffee-like jam from this fruit. The toffee consistency is purely accidental and results from overcooking, but we love it, pulling it into strings like taffy.

We all have a sweet tooth, except for Dad, who does not share our love of the sweet stuff. His preference is salted peanuts, and he eats bags of them. We are chocoholics—Mom, me, Butch, Rabbit, and Queenie. Mom is forced to bury her stash of chocolate bars, like a squirrel hoarding nuts, in the top shelf of the built-in closet in her bedroom, which isn't a perfect hideout. Granted, she does not have a vast selection of hiding places, but even if she owned a combination lock safe, we would find a way to crack it. I have broken my tailbone climbing closets like a monkey. I once drop straight down onto my butt—not at all like a monkey. It doesn't deter me from closet-climbing, though.

One Friday, we are scheduled to leave for Bulawayo for a visit with Ouma and Oupa. That day, we once again raid Mom's closet, looking for chocolates. It's a long trip, and we need to fortify ourselves with sugar before leaving.

"Quickly, Mom will be home soon," Butch says encouragingly, as I dig behind carefully folded items of clothing.

"She'll be coming home early," Rabbit adds.

"Where Daddy?" Queenie asks.

"He's home. Outside, doing some woodwork. Shut up," I respond from the depths of the closet. Dad's woodworking equipment is in the open garage behind the house. "Uh oh, what is this?" My hand comes into contact with what feels like a jar. Pulling it out, we sit down on the floor and examine the mason jar. It is filled with a dark-colored substance. I open the jar and sniff. My sensitive nose detects a fruity, sweet aroma: dried apricots, apples, and something chocolatey. Quickly fetching spoons from the kitchen, we decamp to the safety of our bedroom and devour, spoonful by spoonful, the mysterious substance. It is as tasty as it smells. There is fruit. There is also some unknown, scrumptious taste that we can't quite place, but it vaguely tastes like chocolate.

Since we possess no self-control, we eat until our spoons scrape the bottom of the jar.

We finish just in time, hiding the empty jar under a bed. Tires crunch in the driveway. It is Mom. She never thinks to check the closet to see if the chocolates, or the stuff in the jar, are still there. Dad is in a hurry to get on the road, and we quickly climb into the car. Dad is hoping to reach Bulawayo before sundown.

When Dad drives, his only goal is to reach our destination as quickly as possible. About half an hour into this trip, a stench begins to permeate the car. Dad opens his window, gasping. "Swamp gas! Who farted? Didn't you use the toilet before we left?"

"Yes, Dad," one of us squeaks, "But I need to go again."

We clutch our bellies, groaning in agony. Muttering, Dad finds a place to pull over, and we quickly disappear behind the shrubs and long grass. A few miles further, the funk grows worse, and our pitiful groans louder.

"What did you eat?" Mom asks, shaking her head as she accompanies us into the scrub to relieve our liquid bowels. A frightened informant, I no longer remember who breaks the Omerta Code, telling her we ate the stuff in the bottle in her closet.

"Oh my God!" The horrified look on Mom's face makes our stomachs clench even more. "That's the stuff I got from Auntie Claudia. It's a laxative! Strong, full of cascara and dried fruit. A small teaspoonful is enough to loosen the worst concrete bowel!"

Instead of taking three hours, the rest of the trip takes a full five hours as Dad applies the brakes every few miles so his moaning children can disappear behind a bush. We run out of tissues and are forced to use dried grass and leaves. This mishap does not cure us of our bedroom raids, however, and Mom never learns to stash her goodies in a different place. We don't eat mysterious substances from glass jars anymore, though.

CHAPTER 37

ZIMBABWE RUINS

A legend says that Great Zimbabwe, a vast stone ruin about fifteen miles due south of Fort Vic, was once the capital of the kingdom of Monomotapa. There is a legend, which intrigues me and reminds me of the adventure books by Rider Haggard, that it was visited by the Queen of Sheba. Although that theory is now discounted, I like to think that it is true. Gold had once been mined here — Dad knows this as a prospector — and it is possible in my mind that this is the location of Ophir, King Solomon's gold mines. At age thirteen I am only speculating, of course, and don't pretend to know who built it. The ruins hold so many mysteries that I can believe all the legends even if the archeology does not support them. My connection with this place stretches over many years, and I feel it is far older than anyone knows.

The ruins are our place to go for picnics or day excursions. Long before we move to Fort Vic, the ruins become our favorite spot to visit. I can't remember how old I am when I first see the ruins or climb the hill to the Acropolis, but the site becomes like a second home to us. I am as familiar with it as most people are with their back yards.

I allow my imagination to run riot here. I make up stories about the people who lived here and what their daily lives were like. Some of my stories run to the fantastic, but it only adds to the ruins' mystique and alien nature.

The ruins cover a large area, but the Hill Ruins, the Great Enclosure, and the Valley Ruins are what my family visit the most. The structures are built from mortarless, well-fitting granite blocks, showing a high standard of craftsmanship. The primary enclosures' walls are up to twenty feet thick and thirty-six feet tall, with inlaid granite chevron patterns. It is no surprise the structures have stood for so many ages with little deterioration.

Mom tells me that the Great Enclosure, the main structure in the valley, is shaped like a womb, with a narrow passage that rims the outer wall. In the center of the enclosure stands a solid conical tower, also constructed of granite. No one knows for sure, Mom says, what it represents. Here, she gives me a sideways glance, but I overhear her telling Auntie Claudia when she thinks that I am out of earshot that it is thought to be a phallic symbol. They giggle like schoolgirls. Auntie Claudia says that whoever built it were fertility worshippers, and they giggle again. I don't know what a phallic symbol is, anyway, and I don't understand why it's funny.

The Hill Ruins, or what we call the Acropolis, stands on a granite outcrop overlooking the verdant valley with the present-day ruins below. Butch, Rabbit, and I run up the steep stone steps that lead to the structure on the pinnacle with little effort while the adults, Dad carrying Queenie, labor up the steps, complaining and stopping to rest far too often at the strategically placed, modern stone benches. There are three ways to reach the summit: The Ancient Way, built by the original builders, the Modern Way, and another I no longer remember much about. My preference is the Ancient Way because it is a more challenging climb with narrow steps and tight passages. I squeeze through the passages that twist between enormous granite boulders, my feet carefully negotiating each steep step. I wonder if this challenging ascent has been constructed this way deliberately, for defensive purposes, perhaps? Or, as I speculate with Mom, the builders were tiny people with small feet. No one really knows why the Acropolis was built or what it was used for, she says, since it doesn't have any obvious indication of its purpose.

Our church holds picnics on the grounds, and sometimes we camp out overnight in the valley in areas set aside for picnickers. This place has many happy memories of old friends and idyllic days. It also contains a memory I can't explain.

I am twelve years old when one day, under a dazzling sun, we visit the ruins with the children of Auntie Sadie and Uncle Ruben. James, their African cook, is our chaperone since our parents are busy working or otherwise preoccupied.

"Stay together," James cautions us as we tumble out of the van. I think his face reflects a wariness as he surveys the temple ruins ahead. I wonder if it is the *vadzimu*, his ancestral spirits, that might still inhabit these scattered stone piles that concern him. Or perhaps it is the shaves, the evil spirits that roam the dark corridors looking for easy victims. The ruins, even on this sunny day, have a creepy air about them. Like the legendary shaves, we wander around the temple area for a while, or until we get bored.

"Take us to the Acropolis," we beg James. He frowns. His instructions are to take us to the temple, and it is apparent that he doesn't want to climb up the steep steps.

"You stay near!" he says, shaking his finger, as we reach the base of the hill. "Don't run off. Big leopards up there, and..." he stops, glancing fearfully up at the kopje. We promise, but our promises are worthless.

We race up the steps, shouting and laughing, as poor James puffs behind us, trying to keep up. I can see he is already regretting his temporary nanny job and wants nothing more than to get back to his kitchen. The last place he wants to be is in some spooky, ruined city with a bunch of rowdy, headstrong kids. At last, we reach the summit, with its thick, imposing stone walls. A miombo-tree-forested crown springs up in the gaps between huge boulders that stick up like broken teeth. I want to explore. James is preoccupied with telling one of the other kids to get off the wall. Instead of waiting, I speed through narrow passages, avoiding the highly trafficked areas, to the rear of the hill. Here, tall trees grow amongst craggy boulders, and thick green shrubs make it challenging to get to the lookout spots, but I persist. I can hear James calling in the distance, but I am distracted by an outcropping of massive red boulders I have never seen before. They beckon, and James' call fades as I approach.

I notice a dark, triangular crevice between two of the boulders. I slip through the rift and stop, open-mouthed, in a space high enough for me to stand upright. To my right, there appears to be an opening, a large space between two rocks. Everything is surrounded by rock, and it doesn't look the same as the rest of the outer, blocky ruins. I walk, transfixed, to the open space and peer through it into a smaller room. It is well-lit, as if daylight filters in from somewhere above. On the opposite side of the room, metal pipes run the length of the wall. I've never seen anything like this before in the ruins, and I find myself gaping, fascinated, at what seems to be hieroglyphs carved or etched onto the metal pipes. I want to go up to them and touch them, but just then, I hear James calling again. His voice sounds urgent, so I am forced to stifle my curiosity. I turn back to the entrance, emerging into bright sunlight.

"Where were you?" James demands. "I've been searching all over!" His eyes are wide, fearful. "We must go." He calls for the other children, and we make our way down the hill, and ultimately, home. I never mention my experience, and no one asks.

I do go back later to the Acropolis to search for those boulders and that space between two rocks. I find the location quickly enough, but there is no doorway, only a small crack that I can barely fit into. There is nothing like metal pipes in a room or a space of any description. I indeed possess an active imagination, and I often wonder if I have only imagined all of this. Still, it stands out in my mind to this day with such clarity that I know it was a real experience. James searched for me for a long time and had not thought to look in this opening. Had he even seen it? Where had it gone? I search for it every time I return to the ruins, with no luck. I have since come to the conclusion it doesn't exist. At least, not in this world.

Tea, Scones, and Malaria

CHAPTER 38

AUNTIE GINA, LEON, AND A LEOPARD

I am about twelve when my aunt and cousin from Johannesburg visit: Auntie Gina, Dad's sister, and Leon, her youngest son. We always look forward to their visits. Auntie Gina is a lot of fun and not much like Dad at all. Divorced, she seems cosmopolitan by virtue of living in her own apartment in the center of Johannesburg. I want to grow up to be just like her. A statuesque woman, her blonde hair is piled on her head in a beehive. She wears modish, groovy clothing that says "boutique." No off-the-rack from OK Bazaars or Woolworths. Her sardonic humor tickles me, and Auntie Gina specializes in putting men down. Except for her brothers and five sons, she hates them. I can't blame her. Her ex had been worse than Uncle Harry and Uncle Ruben combined. She converted to Catholicism despite coming from a Protestant family and is a devout Catholic, even though she has been excommunicated from the church for divorcing her husband.

Leon feels like a big brother to us, but he isn't much older than me. Because he has grown up in the city, he isn't familiar with the bush life, but his sophistication and street-savvy impress us. He seems to know so much.

On one of Auntie Gina's and Leon's visits to Fort Vic, we are invited to a wedding. The eldest daughter of Verne and Lenora Knight, the family friends who had taken me to the south coast, is getting married. The wedding is held outside town, at a beautiful home with a large garden nestled between low kopjes. It is owned by the Mathews, family friends from way back in Mom and Dad's past, before we kids were born.

Auntie Gina is an instant hit with the guests, even though she does not know the bride or groom. One can just tell she is no local, and people gather around her like flies around a honeypot, awed at her outfit. This two-piece ensemble looks like a painting by Mondrian. Her carefully tailored suit with the silk-lined jacket hangs on her slim runway-model body. She has put her hair up in her signature style: individual curls that are piled on top of her head. Even though she is in her late forties, she always looks and behaves like a woman in her early thirties.

I am more interested in the food, though, than the clothing people are wearing. Seldom have I seen such a display of *hors d'oeuvres*: pastries, tiny sausage rolls, tarts, bite-size meatballs, and chicken wings... I squat on my heels on the grass between Mom and Auntie Gina sitting in their folding chairs, and each time a tray piled with goodies gets passed around, my arm shoots out from between the chairs. I quickly stuff as much as I can into my mouth before the frowning church lady, giving me the stink-eye, moves on. Mom stares at me, mortified. "You're behaving as if I haven't fed you for a month!" Auntie Gina pretends not to notice but I can see a smile on her face.

"She doesn't have to worry about her weight," she tells Mom, who sniffs. "Let her eat."

At last, I have stuffed my belly enough, and Cousin Leon wanders over.

"Want to explore?" he asks. "I'm bored."

Butch and Rabbit quickly join us, and we head over a nearby kopje behind the house and gardens. Fort Vic is not the bush, and wild animals are rarely seen in the vicinity. The big predators do not venture this close to civilization and we always feel safe wandering around the bush, exploring the rivers, and climbing kopjes and hills.

This one isn't a very big kopje, but we crest it and gaze at the msasa forest stretching out in the valley below. It is spring, and the red, orange, pink, and yellow foliage rivals that of the northern hemisphere's fall colors. Tiny kopjes thrust their rocky heads above the trees, and the warm sun caresses our faces and arms. We descend halfway down the slope and find a smooth spot in which to sit. Leon sighs and removes his shoes. He hates shoes as much as we do. We all take off our shoes and, wiggling our toes, we stretch out on the heated granite rock, looking up at the puffy clouds scudding across the sky.

"That one looks like a dog," someone says.

"No, more like Auntie Lotte. It has her hair, too."

"Can't do this in Jo'burg," Leon says, and he closes his eyes. "Someone would steal the clothes off your back."

I sit, drawing my knees up. I lean back, my hands propping me up, and stare at the edge of the forest below. I hear something. A twig snapping, perhaps? I blink. Then blink again. Movement below. My eyes focus and... I inhale.

Just barely visible, under the msasa tree about thirty feet from us, and next to a large gray boulder, three tiny leopard cubs gambol amongst the dry twigs and leaves. They are so well camouflaged that it is almost impossible to see them, and I must look twice to be sure. My mouth drops open. For a while, it doesn't register that we are in danger. Not until I hear another, much louder, "snap!" and it is then that my heart does a cartwheel and ends up in my throat. A fully grown leopard hidden in the tree above her cubs leaps down onto the leafy ground and turns her golden eyes toward us. She has been there all this time, watching. She takes a step forward, and crouches, her gaze fixed on us as if we are a herd of gazelles.

"Run!" I scream, grabbing my shoes. Rabbit and Butch, galvanized, jump up and grab their shoes, too, as we speed back up the hill. I stop and look around. Leon is not with us. He is still sitting on the rock, frantically attempting to put his shoes back on, his fingers fumbling with the laces. "Run!" I scream again. "Forget the damn shoes!" Finally, city boy leaps up, one shoe on and one shoe off, and hurtles after us. I look back once more as we reach the crest of the hill. Mother Leopard has one kitten in her mouth. I don't look back again. None of us look around. We don't know if Mother Leopard is behind us or only concerned with moving her cubs to a different location. We don't stop to find out, and we keep running until we reach the safety of the wedding party.

Panting, out of breath, we tell anyone in earshot what we have just seen. They gaze at us in disbelief, and finally, Mr. Mathews, along with our pastor, Mr. Brimstone, comes over to speak to us.

"Tell me again, exactly, what did you see?" Mr. Mathews asks. We tell them. Again, and again. They stare at each other, frowns on their faces.

"There are no leopards around here," Mr. Mathews says.

"Maybe it was a civet cat," says Mr. Brimstone, his fingers caressing his handlebar mustache.

A group of men walk behind the kopje to take a look. Returning, they gaze at us kids doubtfully.

"Can't see any sign of a leopard ever having been there," says Mr. Mathews, "and I haven't seen a leopard around here in years, let alone one with cubs."

"It must have been a civet," says another man. Everyone nods, agreeing it is the smaller, less lethal member of the cat family that we've seen. They all decide that it is unlikely a leopard will make her den, along with cubs, so near human habitation. But we kids know what we've seen. We do know what a civet cat is. We also know what a leopard looks like. No one ever believes our story, and many think we've imagined it, seen something else, or lied to get attention.

In retrospect, running is the worst thing we could have done. Cats like to chase stuff, and if it runs, it will become prey. One is supposed to freeze, but all I could think of at the time was getting as far away as I could. Perhaps city boy, by remaining in place, had the right idea, after all.

Combined with the doubt of the adults, I begin to question whether we had seen a leopard at all. Perhaps we have experienced a mass hallucination? It is precisely how I feel about my experience in the ruins, in the strange cavity I had discovered in the rocks. I begin to doubt that too, and now, as an adult, I remember both experiences vividly, but did it really happen? I still don't know.

CHAPTER 39

SHAME, AND A GOOD SAMARITAN

Wild animals are not the only inhabitants of Africa affected by white settlements. The original human tribes, those with darker skins, have, through better or worse, been impacted by our presence. It is when I am twelve, I happen to witness an appalling example of racial injustice, an event that leaves me stunned.

In the 1960s in Rhodesia, racism is a shameful truth. Even as a child, I witness it often, from friends, family, and strangers. At the time, I think it is normal, that this is the way things are, but something deep down in my soul tells me it's wrong.

Racism is an issue that is painful to confront in oneself, and many go through their whole lives living in denial. No one is born with racist ideas or characteristics. Instead, racism is taught, institutionalized, written into law in my own experience, and it becomes a part of society's fabric. Racist behavior in my childhood years is mostly ignored. Looking in the rearview mirror, I can see how it left a scar on my soul that I am still trying to heal. It is said that racism is like living in a cave, and we can choose to come out of it, blinking, into the sunlight of reality. I begin to emerge from my own cave in 1962, the year when the world starts to wake up to the ugly reality of racism in Africa. Algeria, Burundi, Rwanda, have gained their independence from the colonial powers, but in

South Africa, Nelson Mandela has been jailed. In Rhodesia, we think we still have years of white minority rule ahead of us. It would have been wise for our government to, at the very least, become more inclusive, but that doesn't happen until it is much too late, when a terrible civil war becomes the inevitable result.

My memories of Rhodesia are idyllic. Most white Rhodesians still hold this image in their heads of a land of plenty, where prosperity and opportunities once abounded — for whites. True, African tribal people were better off during that period than they currently are, simply because there was stability for a time. The farmers farmed in peace, there was plenty of food and jobs, and even if you were black, you could still survive. But black people never enjoyed the opportunities whites had. Racism had been built into the system.

In 1962 Rhodesia there is an apartheid system. Blacks are not allowed in our schools except as workers. They have separate facilities such as hospitals and restaurants. Even buses have separate seating areas, and in trains, they are confined to "third class" while whites travel first or second class. As a child, I am blissfully unaware of this discrimination, this abomination. I see it, but I don't give it any thought at all. I am so used to it I think of it as normal; the way things are supposed to be.

My wake-up call arrives in 1962, when I witness an incident that leaves a lasting impression on me, one that destroys my view of our perfect society. On a crisp blue and gold day, common in our dry season, I walk home after school. I amble down the dirt road, thinking school-girl thoughts. Maybe I am dreaming about the boy I like in my class: an Italian Adonis named Mario. He never once glances my way, but I always have hope.

As I draw closer to our house, I notice a gray police Land Rover parked in front of our neighbor's home. I bite my lip, my brows drawing together. We never see the law in our neighborhood. There is no crime that I know of, and police, to me, are like little green men from Mars. We hear about them but never see one. I edge over to get a better look. In his light grey shirt and khaki shorts, the policeman, with a peaked cap on his head, stands on the porch. Our neighbor, Mrs. Green, is also there. Her tightly permed curls bob and shake as her voice rises in pitch, but I can't hear what she is saying. Next to her stands a man I recognize as Mrs. Green's houseboy/cook. He is silent, head bowed, hands clasped in front of him.

The policeman is a young white man, perhaps in his early twenties. His arms akimbo, he seems to be questioning the cook. Trying to creep closer, I still can't hear what is being said, but it appears as if the cook denies the charges, shaking his head, as Mrs. Green jabs the air with her finger again and again. The policeman says something to her, and she disappears back into the house.

As I stand on the front lawn, staring, the policeman turns.

"Get out of here," he yells. "This is none of your business."

The beautiful day turns gray and cheerless even though the sun is still out. I am filled with a feeling of foreboding. The policeman faces the cook again, raising his fist. There is a sickening crunch as he strikes the man in the face. The cook wails as blood flies from his nose, spattering on the highly polished concrete porch floor, but his ordeal has only just begun. The cop raises both fists, pummeling the poor man mercilessly. The cook stands his ground, taking every blow as if he knows that things will go much worse for him if he fights back. Our police do not carry guns. Still, they have a lot of power with the law solidly behind them, no matter what, especially when it comes to the African population. It reminds me of my past abuse at the hands of a more powerful woman—Miss Nettles.

At some point, the cop turns around again. I have not moved. "Didn't I tell you to leave?" He is red-faced and tight-lipped. I turn and flee into the safety of my home.

"Mom! There's a policeman hitting Mrs. Green's cook!"

Mom sits serenely at her sewing machine. "Don't look," she says. "He stole money, and she had to call the police. He won't do it again, and she will also fire him."

Whether or not the cook ever steals money again, or to begin with, is not the issue. I feel a strange sensation in the pit of my stomach. A feeling that leaves me nauseous and sick. It doesn't seem fair. Mrs. Green is not a rich woman who keeps thousands of pounds in Rhodesian banknotes in her home. No one is hurt, except for the cook. A few coins, a pound or two, may be missing. Now the cook is being blamed, and justice has been delivered with no legal recourse. I am old enough to know that something isn't right with this picture, but I cannot voice my feelings. It is a scene that I never forget, though, and it stays with me all my life.

How many other black men and women have been violated in this way? I have no idea, but no one seems to care. It is accepted, ignored, and life goes on. Mom is considered a liberal in her political views, yet she does not react to this injustice. She has been taught not to. Compared to what is occurring in South Africa, racial injustice does not seem to be a problem in her adopted country.

Around the same time, Mom sends me to the store on my bicycle. "I want potatoes, tomatoes, and some onions." She hands me enough money to cover the purchases. Mom grew up during the Great Depression, and she knows the price of everything. "Bring back the change." She also knows what I will do with the coins that are left over. I will head straight to the convenience store and buy sweets or to the book store to buy comics. I nod and set off down the road to town.

The town is about two miles away, and I have my own shortcut: down our road to the cut through the bush, past my school on the left, then past the hospital, all on rutted, washboard dirt roads, before I reach the paved roads in town. I lean my bike against the supermarket wall and go inside. Crime is low in our town, and I know the bike will still be there when I come out.

I emerge with a bag crammed with potatoes, onions, and tomatoes. It feels heavy. I balance the bag on the narrow front carrier of my bicycle, ignoring how it bulges over the sides, and pedal back the way I came. Only when I reach the bumpy road near the hospital, an ominous ripping sound puts an end to a so-far uneventful errand. My heart drops down to my feet as onions, potatoes, and tomatoes tumble out, careening in different directions onto the stony dirt road. I throw my bike down with wheels still spinning and frantically begin to gather the produce into my arms. It doesn't take long for me to realize there are simply too many items to carry. My arms are full, and the ripped bag is no longer usable. As I gather up each potato, onion, or tomato, it rolls out of my arms again and boogies down the road, as if mocking me.

I begin to cry. Tears stream down my face and my nose runs like a tap. But I cannot wipe my nose or face. I have no hands free. My bike still lies in the dirt, and if I drop the produce, I can pick up my bike and head home, but then Mom will be angry at me for losing her vegetables. Either way, I can't win. I stand in the middle of the dirt road, sobbing, holding what I can in my arms, which isn't much, staring at my bike and the feckless bag blowing away in the breeze.

"Can I help you, young madam?" A voice says. I turn. A young black man dismounts from his bicycle, pushing it as he walks toward me. "It looks like you are having some trouble."

"Please!" I smile through the tears. "I am in big trouble."

He laughs, places his bicycle down, and helps me gather up the capricious produce. Since we have no bag, he fills his pockets with produce, helps me get my bike upright again, and between the two of us, we cycle, one-handed, armfuls of produce in the other. We have managed to rescue most of it. My spirits rise, and I ask him to follow me home, which he does: an odd duo laden with tomatoes, onions, and potatoes.

When we reach the house, I ask him to wait as I run inside with my armload. I want to reward this man. I want him to have anything in our house that he wishes to have, but I think money would be a more fitting way to express my gratitude for his kindness. I have taken him far out of his way.

"Mom! Can I keep the change?" I ask as I placed the produce onto the kitchen table.

"Why?"

I explain, then add, "And he's waiting out on the road. I want to give him some money for all his trouble."

"Get out of here. You're not getting money. I barely have enough to buy food, and you want to give it away."

It is probably true. My parents are chronically impoverished. To this day, I have no idea where the money goes, but we are always broke. I hand her the change and walk slowly outside, my head hanging in shame.

"My Mom won't give me money," I tell the young man, "but I want to thank you for your help. I won't forget it."

And I don't forget it. The man cycles off, whistling. He doesn't look offended. He is probably used to the white man's ways, and it most likely doesn't surprise him at all. I feel the help comes from his heart, and not because he expects a reward. The universe does not forget, and I hope providence has since repaid him a thousand-fold for his kindness toward a desperate child. I consider him an angel, sent by God.

I also believe that my parents remain insolvent because they grew up in the Depression, but they are trapped in a cycle of poverty and lack. This condition comes from their parents. It is a normal state of being for both of them. Dad is a talented builder who can make better earnings working for the right company, yet he sticks with his government job. Mom undervalues her talents, as does Dad. Neither of them believes they deserve better in life because they have been conditioned this way. They pinch every penny twice before parting with it. Yet, their generosity knows no bounds when it comes to scoundrels and con artists.

CHAPTER 40

THE GOLD MINE CAPER

It appears as if Mom and Dad's dream of financial solvency has begun to manifest. With Mom's job, and the house and other debts getting paid off, there is a glimmer of daylight on the horizon. But in 1962, Dad enters into a catastrophic business deal that, within a year, leaves us bankrupt and my parents desperate.

For some time, Dad has shown an interest in amateur prospecting. Rhodesia is rich in minerals, gold, and gemstones. While on the bush job, he prospects in his spare time and returns home with small gold nuggets, or tiny emeralds still encased in the ore. Pulling them out of his pocket, he hands them to us, and we play with them. He never cashes these in, but he is convinced he has found a rich deposit of gold near Fort Vic. I am unsure whether he purchases the land or only receives a license to mine on the land. My memory is not clear, but I feel it is the latter.

We visit the mine on weekends. I inspect the impressive set-up, high bankers, and sluicers that separate the gold from the lumps of gravel. Dad digs all day, by himself, while we roam the area. When we return, he has a pile of gravelly, pulverized quartz ready to place on the equipment. He runs water over the bed of gravel from collected rainwater in barrels. This works well in the rainy season, and we help him with the hose, one end in the barrel, and the other over the sluicer. Sometimes he'll discover a tiny speck of gold, but never anything that will indicate anything significant.

"There's gold here, I know there is," he says repeatedly. "It's not deep, like the Rand in Johannesburg. It's lying on the surface. If I can just find enough to pay for the mine equipment, we can expand and dig deeper. I can hire men, and more equipment..."

I hope that Dad will strike gold. I want to be rich. I want him and Mom to stop worrying about money, to stop pinching pennies. I want a watch on my wrist like my friends wear, new clothes, and all the comics I can read. I want my own horse. I am tired of being driven around in old cars that leak and break down regularly.

Then Dad enters into a business partnership with a man I'll call Sydney Lumpkin, an amateur prospector. "He'll help me to work on the mine. He can also contribute financially." Lumpkin is a rangy man with greasy hair that hangs over a cheerless, bilious face, a clear warning that Sydney lives to drink. His diminutive, whey-faced wife, Enola, wears a perpetual expression of hopelessness. Mom always says Enola is so passive she can't say boo to a goose. When they visit our home for a meal, her brood of seven children, all boys, attacks the food as if someone will snatch it away from them. Enola sadly mentions that they don't have money to buy food. Sydney, we discover later, spends it all on booze. "My boys need school uniforms," Enola adds, "And I can't pay for them. The school won't allow them in without uniforms." Through first-hand experience, I know this to be true. My heart aches for the Lumpkins, as does Mom's.

Since Mom has a job now at Meikles, she asks her boss, the store manager, if Mrs. Lumpkin can buy groceries and clothes for her children on our account. He agrees but stipulates Mom and Dad will be responsible for making the payments. Dad has also purchased even more mining equipment, thinking Mr. Lumpkin will pay for half, which he has agreed to do. But as it turns out, Sydney does not contribute a bean. The new equipment eats up all Mom and Dad's hard-earned savings, and Mom begins to have her doubts about the Lumpkins.

"Have you made him sign anything?" she asks Dad one evening while we are eating dinner.

"It's not necessary," he says. "Sydney is an honorable man. He'll stick to the verbal agreement." But his face tells us otherwise. Dad is beginning to have his doubts, too. As if to convince himself, he adds, "He's just down on his luck at the moment. His job has been messing him around and they don't pay him what he's worth. And once we find gold..."

Mom's face is a picture of misgiving. "I hope so. They haven't paid back a penny for the clothes and food they've bought on our account."

Month after month, the store bill for food and groceries mount, and still Mr. Lumpkin does not pay. My parents are having a difficult time making even minimum payments. Every time Dad confronts Sydney about the money situation, he comes up with an excuse. "My wife is sick. I have to pay the doctor." Enola looks worn enough to lend some legitimacy to this claim. Sydney has a job, but he trots out the old "I haven't been paid yet" regularly. Like the loaves and the fishes, though, his whiskey supply never runs out. Dad is a soft touch for any con man. To boot, Dad remains a poor businessman, and Sydney and his wife know it. They can coast through several more months without repaying a brass copper. I guess Sydney hopes he and Dad will strike it rich, and then all his problems will be solved.

The mine runs into problems—big ones. There is no water on the mine. It doesn't rain often enough, and Dad has sunk several boreholes with no luck. Perhaps Dad should have already known this, but I am not privy to what is going through Dad's head at this time. Poor decisions and lack of running water ensure the mine's fate. Even had there been a mother lode of gold in the ground, they could not retrieve it without enough running water. Dad continues with his job out in the bush. One week when Dad is away in the bush working his ass off, Sydney Lumpkin sells the mining equipment for what he can get for it and absconds with his wife, kids, and the money. To where no one knows. No one ever sees the Lumpkins again. Dad is left holding the debt owed on the equipment and the astronomic store bill. He has no choice but to sell the house and to find another job that will help him pay off his debts. Life is about to get rocky again.

PART III

THE TREMULOUS TEENS

1963 — 1968

Tea, Scones, and Malaria

CHAPTER 41

ROCKY ROADS

1963

The most remembered day in world history must be November 23, 1963. It is a Saturday, and we are visiting Auntie Sadie. Axel, Ellie-May, Butch, and I rise early to go horse riding, and now we have just returned to the farmhouse. As we walk up the steps to the verandah, Auntie Sadie meets us.

"President Kennedy has been assassinated! He's dead." Her face is white, brown eyes wide with shock.

Axel asks, "Who's he?" Except for Axel, we all know who Kennedy is. We stand on the verandah for a while, absorbing this information. Although it happened yesterday, our evening, we'd not had the radio on, so it is only the next day when the news arrives on the farm. Although I am not an American at the time, the event has an impact on me. Again, except for Axel perhaps, we all admire Kennedy, and we've learned about him in school.

That year, 1963, is another life-changer for us. Since Dad has lost the mine and still owes on mining equipment that he no longer possesses, and the store where we shop will no longer allow us to buy on credit, Mom and Dad are left with little choice. They must sell the house and start again. I am not sure if they declare bankruptcy, but I doubt it. Their pride will not allow them to do that. They most likely decide that they will pay back every penny they owe, and the creditors are knocking at our door.

One day Dad and Mom call us all into the living room.

"I've resigned the government job," Dad says, "and I've found a position with Rebar Construction. I start in a few months. We're moving."

"Where?" I ask when I find my voice. I am in my second year of high school. I've made friends, and I'm doing well in most subjects. Okay, not math or science, but still.

"The Lowveld," Mom says, her voice at its smile-at-all-costs inflection. Before we can ask, Dad continues.

"The Lowveld is where we lived in Nuanetsi, but we're not going there. It's a different part of the Lowveld, closer, but still far from here. I will be building canals for the new sugar estates."

"The bad news is," Mom says, "You'll all be going to boarding school. But not Queenie," she adds hastily. "She's still too young. I'll teach her."

"*Th-that* school? The one I went to..."

"Yes. That school. They've improved, I hear." Mom's smiley voice comes out again. "And...wait for it...Auntie Claudia is sending Rosa, Paloma, and Livia there too. And Georgia. You'll have friends!"

"We're going back to the bush life again," Dad says, "So it won't be easy with the schools. There isn't any way your mother can teach all of you, and we'll be moving around for the first few years. There's not much in the way of housing, again. We'll be camping."

We look at each other. We like camping. The school, though, makes us nervous. I don't really want to leave, but it's clear we have no choice. Mom seems, on the surface, to be okay with everything, but the failure of the mine, the upcoming move back to the bush, and the still outstanding debt is weighing on her. It is the first time I see Mom suffer debilitating bouts of depression. She locks herself in her bedroom, pleading a migraine, but I can hear her sobbing through the door. I feel helpless and frightened. It becomes so bad I fear she will kill herself. I don't know where I get this notion from, but it is probably from all the adult books I read. One day I come home from school to find her locked again behind her bedroom door.

I bang on the door. Mom yells at me to go away. *Why? Why has she locked her door? She never does this.* I panic. I am the only one at home besides her, and I don't know what I should do. That morning when I leave for school, I am afraid to leave her. It occurs to me I can go to the window and peek in. If she is going to kill herself, I will be able to run to the neighbor and get help, but first, I need to know if my worst fears are materializing. I creep around to the bedroom window and peer over the sill, through the open louvered window, only to meet the outraged eyes of Mom as she sits in front of her sewing machine.

"I asked you to go away," she says through clenched teeth. Her eyes are red and watery. She throws down a doll's dress that she has been sewing. "I wanted to surprise you! Now you've spoiled the surprise."

In tears, I skulk away from the window. But at least I know. Mom is not about to kill herself. I don't think Mom realizes her moods are evident to at least one of her children or that I am afraid of what she may do to herself. Her pain makes her impervious to my worry. I don't know if my sisters or brother are aware of this situation; I only know I am acutely aware of it. It brings a pall over my life. I find out later that she has suffered depression and migraines most of her life, but she can conceal it from us and can function normally most times. Only when life throws her curveballs will she retreat into herself and try to shut life out. I inherit her migraines, and I wonder if this is our way of coping with stress.

I too dread my return to boarding school. I am happy in our government school, looking forward to my second year of high school, and, for a change, doing well academically. Butch and Rabbit are not delighted, either, but we have no choice. We are enrolled in the boarding school in Gwelo for the year of 1964.

CHAPTER 42

SCHOOL, AND PREDATORS

1964

In 1964 Ian Smith becomes our new Prime Minister. The Federation of Rhodesia and Nyasaland dissolves and we are now, as a country, walking in lockstep toward a civil war. Elsewhere in the world, the Rolling Stones make their debut album and Cassius Clay changes his name to Muhammad Ali.

After the Christmas holidays are over, Mom drives us to Gwelo in her Consul that is beginning to look like a piece of old space junk that has returned to earth. I am still thirteen, Butch is going on twelve, and Rabbit is nearly ten. I feel somewhat comforted this time, knowing my brother, sister, and friends are with me. I figure it can't be as bad as I remember. At least this time I don't feel as if I am being abandoned by my family. We are all in the same storm and will support each other.

Mom packs up or sells what we can't take to the bush with us, which is almost everything, and joins Dad at our new campsite in the Lowveld while we are driven to the school by family friends.

The school has changed. The small dormitory I was in before is now the boy's dorm, and the girl's dorm is a new building on the opposite side of the property. High school girls share a room with one other girl, and the younger girls, which include Butch, are placed in a communal dormitory with bunk beds. I feel better already. I share a room with a girl I shall call Angela, a pretty girl from Salisbury. She is messy, but so am I. We get along well, discovering we have the same sense of humor and sassiness.

Every week our dorm mother, Auntie Iris, does an inspection. Our room always fails the assessment. Angela and I are assigned tasks such as floor scrubbing, toilet cleaning, or bath scouring as punishment. I quickly learn to become an over-achiever in house cleaning. I even find I enjoy it. Our favorite task is to soap the long, tiled corridor in the middle of the dorm. We pour buckets of water onto the floor, skating or sliding on our bare feet from one end to the other until the floor shines. We mop it all up before Auntie Iris is any the wiser.

I love being with my old friends from Fort Vic, and I make more friends quickly. Although our principal Mr. Tenenbaum is a strict man, he, at least, doesn't believe in corporal punishment. We have nothing to fear. He assigns hard labor for miscreants. I find myself doing hard labor quite frequently, such as weeding the vegetable garden. I enjoy this, too, since I always have plenty of company. We eat carrots from the garden when we are hungry, which, unfortunately, is often.

The school has not improved in the food department. The wife of the principal is in charge of the kitchen. We name her Eagle Eyes. She rakes the dining room with eyes that remind me of the cobra eyes of Miss Nettles, but she is more like a bird of prey. She even looks like one, with her hook nose. We are like mice in her talons. She never smiles, and if she catches one of us flouting her rules, she pins us with a gaze that would freeze a leopard in its tracks. That is all she needs to do. The food is, at best, inconsistent. On weekends, it tends to be prepared more thoughtfully than the weekly menu, which often includes a gray casserole made up of Sunday leftovers. Vegetables are cooked until mushy, as if we are toothless octogenarians in a nursing home. The school still adheres to its vegetarian policy and does nothing to improve the tasteless slop's nutritional quality. I am still always hungry and dream of food. On our monthly excursions into town, our pocket money, *aka* church tithe, all too quickly is spent on meat pies at the local café. These monthly visits to the fleshpots must be earned by good behavior.

When I turn fourteen, my creativity begins to stir and will not be silenced. I write plays, produce and star in them, and these begin to gain popularity in the school. Even the principal attends, which is surprising since my writings are not religious in nature.

Angela morphs into a troubled girl, and I can never figure out what is going on with her. She launches into hysterical fits of sobbing for no apparent reason. We are all teenagers, complicated and overly dramatic, but Angela takes the drama to a new level.

The following year I leave this school. They are not set up for my last two years of high school. I overhear my parents discussing what has happened during my last year there. After Mr. Tenenbaum retires, we get a new principal, a pastor. We admire this man and love his sermons. His wife and kids are all at this school. He is a role model for us, and what I overhear shocks me to my core. This man has molested some of the girl students—my friends. It suddenly all makes sense. Angela's moods, her crying jags... I am horrified. This is when my religious upbringing begins to take on a different tone. Although I have somehow escaped this fate, I feel like a spiritual rug has been pulled out from under my feet.

I am not unfamiliar with predators. During my first year at this school, Rabbit and I are sent back after the holidays by train. I don't remember where Butch is. Perhaps she has been staying with friends who will return her to the school, but Rabbit and I are on the train to Gwelo, the one that leaves from Mbizi siding. The siding is about half an hour's drive from our camp in the Lowveld, and it stops here to pick up the boarders returning to boarding schools in Gwelo and Bulawayo.

Rabbit and I have a compartment to ourselves. When the train pulls out of the siding, I leave our compartment and go into the corridor to look out the window. I notice a man standing at the next window, leaning out with his elbows on the sill. He is in his thirties, I guess, and he turns as I approach. "How old are you?" he asks me, out of the blue.

"Thirteen."

He smiles, but the smile does not extend to his eyes. "You look younger." I am uncomfortable immediately. "Are you alone?"

"No, my brother is with me." I point to the compartment, where Rabbit still sits.

The man walks to the door, looks in, and enters, perching on the seat across from Rabbit. He begins to talk. Not knowing what else to do, I sit down next to Rabbit.

"I'm a teacher," he tells us. He is on his way to a school in Northern Rhodesia (now Zambia). I ask him some questions about his school, and he answers them in a friendly way, but I don't like how his cold eyes never leave me. They are intense, cobalt blue, but they remind me of shark eyes. After some more chit-chat, he rises and stands, arms folded across his chest. He glances at my now terrified brother. "Get out." His head indicates the door, and he moves to one side, but stands in front of me, blocking my exit.

Rabbit makes as if to rise, but I clutch his arm. "Stay! Don't leave." My fingers dig into his arm. I don't let go. To Rabbit's credit, he does not move another muscle, although I can tell he is as paralyzed by fear as I am. I am nauseous. What can I do? I am still a skinny, knock-kneed child small for my age, and Rabbit is even smaller. The man waits, but we sit as if glued to our seat. He asks Rabbit to leave again. Rabbit shakes his head. After giving a disgusted snort, he turns and leaves. We do not see him again for the entire trip, but sadly, we do not tell an adult. This man probably finds another victim since the train is full of returning school kids. At that time, we are not equipped to deal with the situation since we've never been warned about predators. The most I've ever been told is never to accept sweets from a stranger. This man is not offering sweets.

Although we return to the bush for school holidays, it is no longer the idyllic life we once led in Nuanetsi.

Tea, Scones, and Malaria

CHAPTER 43

THE LOWVELD

One of our camps near Chiredzi. Pie, Queenie, Rabbit, and Butch, in chair.

D uring school vacations, which occur roughly three times a year for three weeks, we travel home by train to Mbizi, where Mom picks us up in her Consul that still runs, gasping and wheezing over the rutted dirt roads, refusing to quit and go into a junkyard retirement.

I am jarred by our first encampment, a testament to how far I have shifted into a different cultural attitude. A makeshift construct that looks more like a homeless shelter crouches under an acacia in a sea of mopane and knobby thorn trees. A freshly constructed irrigation canal filled with soupy green water is a short distance from our camp. Dad is in the process of building more canals, a network that will eventually crisscross the sugar estates. Dad says crocodiles lurk in their muddy depths, and we are to stay away from the canals. Sometimes we obey, but we dangle our feet in the sluggish flow on hot days.

Our campsite makes me long for our tin shack in Nuanetsi. Dad has bought a small camper (or caravan, as we locals call them) with what is left over from the sale of our house in Fort Vic. A tarp slung over a rough framework of poles makes for a shady respite from the blazing sun. A thatched pole shelter becomes our dining room, and where Mom teaches Queenie her first year of correspondence school. The kitchen is a concrete slab with a corrugated tin roof propped up on rough bark poles. On the slab sits our familiar old wood stove. The small tin shack that had once been Dad's workshop and his bedroom on job sites is now our bathroom. Like the return of an old friend, the tin tub awaits us inside. Dented, with rusty spots, it has seen better days. Dad has patched it up with his soldering iron, ready for use.

Our camp here is temporary since no housing is yet available for us. We know, though, we will be living this way for some time to come, moving from place to place like nomads as Dad's job sites change.

Petina remains with us, along with Johnny M'barro, who toddles naked around the campsite. Dad constructs quarters for them behind our makeshift camp. Petina takes hardship in her stride as if the lovely house with running water and electricity was all a dream, and we are now awake again in the real world.

Dad has disposed of the Siddeley. The construction company has loaned him a bakkie.

The general area with the sugar cane and two sugar mills is known as Hippo Valley. When Dad has finished constructing the canals, his company is commissioned to build the town of Chiredzi. Chiredzi means "fish hook" in the local language. It mushrooms out like a gold-rush town as more and more people, lured by the promise of an economic boom, begin to settle the area. The fast-growing town spreads out under the backdrop of a towering conical hill dotted with baobab trees.

Our nearest campsite neighbor is a recluse named Sam, a wizened man of indeterminate age. I think he looks like an over-cured strip of biltong wearing shorts and a tank top. A cigarette hangs from his dry lips, and when we try to talk to him we only get a "Harumph!" in return.

"He drinks, and he's crazy," Dad says. "Stay away from him."

We do. Sam lives rough, much the same as us, and he also drives a bakkie. We can see his camp and the bakkie through the trees. One day, as we sit under our lean-to shelter in front of the caravan, we are startled by an explosion that shakes the ground. A plume of sooty smoke rises above the mopane and thorn trees, and orange flames flicker from the direction of Sam's camp.

"Stay here!" Dad shouts as he runs over to Sam's camp. We wonder what has happened. Did Sam's propane tank blow up? We can hear Dad's shouts through the trees, but we can't see anything. After a while, the flames die down, a thin trickle of smoke and an acrid smell the only evidence something transpired. Dad finally returns, shaking his head.

"What happened?" we ask in unison.

"Sam's the drunkest I've ever seen him," Dad replies. "He says he tried to start the bakkie, and it wouldn't start, so he picked up a can of petrol, doused it, then threw a match. There's nothing left of the bakkie. With the help of his cook, I made sure the fire was extinguished and we put Sam to bed. He can sleep it off. Tomorrow, he'll probably wonder what the hell happened to his vehicle."

Mom and Dad both come from this type of background. They find it difficult to see this behavior as abnormal or dysfunctional. To them, it is how people are. They are accustomed, inured, to it.

Our holidays at home mean rough living, with no electricity, running water, or any semblance of civilization that we've become used to. We sweat out the hot nights in our caravan, placing wet washcloths on our faces to stay cool. It doesn't help. We can't sleep outside. We need mosquito netting over the beds to protect us not only from mosquitoes but spiders and other insects. Thanks to the stagnant water in the canals, mosquitoes are abundant, and we are back to the malaria prophylactics. We still pretend to take them, then spit them out later. I never get malaria again, and my siblings also seem to be magically protected from the bush diseases.

To stay entertained, we write plays and produce them on an eight-track tape recorder. This is not much of an improvement over our Moses production, but we have fun with it on the sweltering days when it's too hot to venture out.

We write horror plays complete with creaking doors, thunder, horses' hooves, or whatever sound effects the plots call for. We discover a flexible tin sheet that makes a perfect peal of thunder, and we drum our fingers on the tabletop for horse's hooves. A cabinet door in the caravan suffices for the door effect.

We name our creations *The Creaking Door*, purloined from the RBC Radio show with the same name. We don't feel guilty about pilfering its title. We itch to use the signature eerie creak to introduce every play we produce, and since our setting is always a dark and stormy night, we sprinkle crashes of thunder liberally throughout the play. The plots do not need to make sense. We once again argue over who gets the plum parts. Dracula, Frankenstein, The Mummy…all are the coveted roles. Christopher Lee, Boris Karloff, and Bela Lugosi are not a patch on our efforts.

In the evenings, Dad teaches us to play poker. Instead of money, which is still in short supply, we use matchsticks. Poker and chess are some of our favorite games, along with Monopoly and Scrabble.

I spend all my pocket money, still a rarified thing in our lives, on books. Mom and I are both hooked on murder mysteries, suspense, and horror. Mom now does not mind me reading her books. She is broad-minded when it comes to movies and reading. On some of our trips to Bulawayo, she'll take me to see PG-rated films and demand they let me in. They do. I see quite a few Hitchcock movies this way.

At last, Dad finishes with the canals. Now that his company has been contracted to build the necessary infrastructure in the town of Chiredzi, we will move closer to the town. His assignments will include building a supermarket, a bank, and Town Council offices. Also, a hospital. The town is growing quickly as people move in to farm sugar, cotton, and citrus. We are still in the bush, though, still living primitively. There are no permanent homes available for us yet.

CHAPTER 44

CAMP FOLLOWERS

Queenie has always loved chickens.

Mom and Dad decide to keep chickens again. Chiredzi still does not have a supermarket, and we must drive many miles to find a good butcher. Our chicken run is behind the caravan, and Dad incubates eggs, which gives us some good laying hens, roosters, and some for the pot.

Queenie has adopted one of the chickens, a tiny black scrap of feathers who stands out from all the other yellow chickens in the run. She calls her our "go-to" name, "Blackie," just like the black cat we'd once had in Nuanetsi.

Blackie follows Queenie everywhere, and she considers Queenie her mom. She grows into a fat, contented hen, but she and Queenie are still inseparable.

It is a Sunday morning, and we are all home for the school holidays. Mom tells the young lad Dad has hired to take care of the chickens and do various odd jobs around the camp to slaughter a chicken for the Sunday dinner. If we'd been paying attention, we'd have noticed which one the young man found rather easy to catch. Blackie is the low-hanging fruit of the chicken run.

Mom has discovered the awful truth much too late, but what can she do? We refuse to eat a morsel of food that day, going hungry rather than cannibalizing our dear friend. Mom grew up during the Great Depression, and she doesn't believe anything should go to waste. Not even Blackie.

Despite the terrible loss, Queenie befriends other chickens, highlighting how flexible our family must be to survive rough bush-living. Our situation does not improve over the next year. Gypsy-like, we live in several camps like this one, all much the same design and configuration. We move every few months, following the canals, and each time we come home from boarding school, we find ourselves in a new camp.

The cats we acquired in Fort Vic, Bo-Peep and her daughter Lady Gray, along with Butch's dog Spooky, come with us. The cats become half-feral and produce a litter of kittens every year. We do our best to find homes for them, populating the Lowveld with the offspring. Bo Peep and Lady Gray always locate a hollow tree trunk to give birth, and sometimes we find it, but most often not. They guard their litters fiercely.

A popular dog in Rhodesia is the Ridgeback. They are large dogs, with a signature ridge along the spine. Used as hunting dogs, they are fearless. One day, a family friend arrives at our camp with two of his Ridgebacks sitting in the bed of his bakkie. As the vehicle pulls up in our campground, the dogs bound out, tongues lolling, to greet us. Seconds later, two furious furballs, Bo Peep and Lady Gray descend upon the unwary dogs, landing on their heads with claws extended. The mother cats have kittens in the vicinity. Buckets of water are hastily brought to get the cats off the dogs. No one wants to get involved in the maelstrom of claws, flying fur, and teeth. The howling dogs, their heads a bloody mess, leap back into the bakkie and cower there, refusing to emerge for the duration of the visit. Although they are torn up and bloodied, they do recover from the attack. The cats are okay. We observe them sitting under a tree, licking their paws in satisfaction.

It is impossible to live in the bush and ignore the wildlife around us. One morning, a baby duiker, a small antelope, bounds into our camp, where it becomes trapped inside the thatched room. Dad says she must have been separated from her mother, who has possibly fallen prey to a predator. I try to feed her milk from a bottle with a teat, but she won't come near me. I try giving her grass, but she rears up, her sharp little hooves slashing the air. I long to keep her, but she strongly objects to being my pet and escapes her imprisonment the same night. I reluctantly allow her to run — we just aren't equipped to take care of a wild animal — but I cry all night because I don't think she'll survive.

Not all our visitors are so benign. One night, we return home from the club after watching a movie. It is dark, and the car's headlights light up the campground as we pull in. A dark mass on the ground, about the size of a man's hand, rears up, eight eyes glittering in the beam. Amidst the screams coming from inside the car, and even Dad's horrified gasps, we can still hear the hissing of the tarantula as it prepares to defend itself from the blaze-eyed monster.

"Stay in the car," Dad orders, quite unnecessarily. No one is moving. "I'm not killing this thing with my shoe." Sprinting to the caravan, he retrieves his rifle from the lockbox inside. Quickly loading it, he runs back to the middle of the camp. The spider is still up on its hind legs, its forelegs waving in the air. Dad is a good shot, and this night, he dispatches the spider efficiently and mercilessly. Trembling, we get out of the car and make our way around the splattered remains of this horror. It is not poisonous, but it is terrifying, and we don't want it roaming our camp. It is most likely a greater horned baboon tarantula, which can grow to a span of five inches. This one is every bit of that and perhaps more.

Despite being a pragmatic man who understands the harshness of the bush and only kills when he feels he has little choice, Dad has a soft heart, especially when it comes to birds. Except for Queenie's hen Blackie, and our dog and cats, our pets are destined to be of the more exotic variety.

CHAPTER 45

HUEY AND DEWEY

Our final camp seems almost luxurious compared to the first two or three. We still have the caravan, the lean-to kitchen, and the tin hut bathroom, but now there is an extra room—a crude, rectangular pole and *ðaga* (mud) hut topped off by an untidy thatch roof. Sheets of corrugated iron patch up the sides, but there are still gaping spots in the walls where one can drive a bakkie through. At least this shelter is cooler than the caravan.

The marula trees surrounding the camp drop fruit that we gather so Mom can make her infamous jam that doubles as our toffee treat. We search for monkey orange trees or monkey bread trees to nosh on in our Eden. Monkey oranges, hard fruit with pulpy, orangey-brown, tangy pits, are our favorite. The monkey bread, or camel-foot, is a tree with an enormous flat pod that is mostly edible.

My favorite tree, beside the baobab, is the lucky bean tree, or red-hot poker tree. However, one must be cautious around it since the brilliant coral-red flowers attract African killer bees. What attracts me to these trees is not its flower, but the seed. It bears flat pods filled with coral-red beans. I gather these beans and make jewelry from them. What I don't know at the time, and maybe none of us do, is that these beans are deadly, containing a similar toxin to curare. Though one

247

must eat them to suffer ill effects, we still flirt with death daily in the bush, and a few toxic beans do not stop our activities.

We are now in a denser part of the bush, with taller trees and thick scrub. The bush is never silent. We have a daily chorus of bird song. Emerald doves with their "ask father" coo, the gray lourie with its nasal *kweh* or "go away" cry, the yellow-billed hornbill's cluck-clucking, and the constant background ensemble of smaller birds, frogs, and cicadas. Days and nights are filled with sound.

Some of Dad's workers discover a hornbill nest at the job site, removing two baby hornbills not yet able to fly. Dad knows that these little birds will become someone's snack unless he intervenes. He demands that his workers give him both birds, so they do. I think there is also some monetary compensation. He brings them home, and Dad hand-feeds these birds with a slurry of ground beef and water. He keeps them with him, even at night. They become his babies, and he names them Huey and Dewey after Donald Duck's boys.

To everyone's amazement, Huey and Dewey survive to grow into healthy adult birds. The adult hornbill is about the size of a parrot, gray with spotted black and white feathers. It has an enormous hooked yellow bill that seems too large for its body and is often called a "flying banana." (In the movie *The Lion King* it is a character named Zazu.)

As the hornbills grow, ground beef alone is no longer adequate. They need insects, and they have not been taught to forage for their own food. They cannot fly, either. Dad has clipped their wing feathers. When we are home from school, we are doomed to feed these birds. Dad sends us kids out into the bush every day to catch grasshoppers or any other insect we can find. We take a glass mason jar and a net and stalk grasshoppers, termites, crickets, and cicadas for hours. When we don't have grasshoppers or we are at school, the two birds hop around on the ground around the camp, looking for insects. The cats and Spooky leave them alone. Sometimes they'll be fed small bits of beef, fruit, or nuts. Whatever their diet, though, they thrive.

Huey and Dewey go everywhere with Dad—to work, to the Hippo Valley Estates Club, sitting on his shoulder while he watches movies or plays golf. He feeds them popcorn or peanuts. They go shopping with him, or wherever he decides to go. They are always on his shoulders and never leave his side. Dad is well-known around the area for his tame hornbills, and people tolerate their messy, chattering presence. I can't recall how long he has these birds, though, perhaps a year. Hornbills can have a 20-year lifespan, and I know Dad does not have them that long. Maybe he decides they can take care of themselves in the bush, and he releases them. I am sure that decision cannot have been easy for him, but he makes it while we are at school. When we return home, they are gone.

Tea, Scones, and Malaria

CHAPTER 46

A STORM, A RIVER, AND A CASHEW

We do enjoy breaks from bush life. We often travel to our nearest beach, Beira, a coastal city in Mozambique. It is our neighboring country and, at that time, a colony of Portugal. Most Rhodesians come here for their holidays, and we are no exception.

I love the beach. Mom has grown up on the coast, and she needs her infusion of beach and ocean as often as we can manage it. In other years, we go south to the fantastic beaches in South Africa, along the Cape and the Natal coasts. There is hardly a year when we do not make a trip to a beach somewhere. Dad is less enthusiastic. His idea of a vacation isn't getting sand in your shorts. He prefers to visit family, so we are often forced to stop and visit aunts, uncles, and cousins en route. However, Mom ensures these visits remain as short as possible.

Beira is the one place where we have no family. So Dad hates Beira.

"It's full of damn Portuguese," he says, as we stop at a filling station to fill up the car. "I can't speak their language, and if another one of the men peers in at the girls, I'll..." He doesn't finish, but I cringe.

"Are they human?" Rabbit pipes up from the back seat.

Tea, Scones, and Malaria

"Of course they are. They just speak a different language, that's all," I say, annoyed by my family.

Dad also dislikes Portuguese men because they become pests once we enter our teenage years. We shoo them away regularly, using Portuguese words we've learned: *sumir* (scram), or sometimes *vamoo*, which we think is Portuguese, but it's not. Still, they gather around us on the beach like flies at a picnic. Regardless of the lotharios, none of us can say anything bad about the food.

Portuguese food is divine; Portuguese mixed with Mediterranean with an African flair—so different from what we are used to. It is cheap enough so we can afford to eat well here. We often go out to dine because it is less expensive than eating in. For the price of a *cerveza* (beer) or two, we receive plates of tapas—beans, spicy marinated chicken livers, olives, bread, and cheese—enough to fill the stomachs of a family of six. If we are extra hungry, we order a *piri-piri* (an African chili) chicken—a whole roasted chicken to divide amongst the family. No one drinks the cerveza, but we polish off the tapa dishes down to every last crumb or bite.

My first vacation in Beira is in 1960 when I am nine years old. Ouma often comes with us, but our first visit includes Oupa. It is the last time he goes anywhere with us on vacation. His health is already beginning to deteriorate.

We stay at the Estoril campgrounds, a complex of chalets that sprawl to the beach, now called Makuti Beach. At the far end, a red and white-banded lighthouse rises, its beams piercing the night sky. We can't afford to stay in the hotels, but the spartan chalets are inexpensive. We have bunk beds, and I always choose the top bunk so I can look out a little window at the ocean less than a hundred yards away. I lie awake at night, listening to the crash and thunder of the waves. I can't wait for morning to arrive. As soon as the first sliver of an orange sun peeks over the horizon, casting a golden sheen on the blue water, I slide out of my bunk, pull on my swimsuit, and am out of the door before anyone is awake. I'll soon be in the water, frolicking in the surf like a seal. Mom must always send one of my siblings to bring me back for breakfast. As soon as I bolt the food down, I am out of the door again.

The beach is a delight. At one end stands an old, rusted-out wreck of an ancient fishing vessel. It isn't big, but in my mind, it is what is left of the Titanic. Most of it is missing, and the rest lies half-buried in the sand. I sit inside the wreck and make up stories about the wreck in my head. It is a pirate boat, and it meets its end during a pitched battle between Spanish galleons and other pirates. No, not a pirate boat anymore, but now an ocean liner, and I am the captain. I am sending Morse code—I tap it out on a rusty girder sticking up out of the sand. *Send help. Sinking.* I prefer the pirates, though. My sword is a driftwood piece, and I smack it on the hull, daring Blackbeard to board my ship. I am making my escape now, running down to the breakers and diving in. In my mind, I am half-drowned, and I allow the gentle waves to wash me up on a strange shore—a desert island—Makuti Beach.

The more mundane reality is that this boat has been deliberately grounded on the beach to serve as a breakwater.

This year, we experience an unforgettable storm that hits Beira early one morning with no warning. The howling wind is like a wild animal screaming around our chalet, determined to get under the flimsy roof that groans and trembles with each gust. Flashes of lightning make us close our eyes and hide our faces, and with each peal of thunder the ground trembles under our feet. The water sloshes around our little chalet and we fear it will wash us away. Mom and Ouma drag us under the dining room table, while Dad and Oupa stand at the window, counting the chalet roofs as the wind rips them off, tumbling end over end down the beach.

"There goes another one!" Dad exclaims.

"That makes five now," Oupa replies.

"*God in hemel*, save us," Ouma loudly prays, reverting to her native Afrikaans. "Don't let our roof blow off too!"

At last, the storm subsides, and we emerge from our chalet to survey the wreckage. Shells of chalets still stand, most without a roof, and many are waterlogged. People pack up their vehicles, making ready to cut their vacations short. Except for our chalet and a few others, there is almost nothing left of the Estoril Camp Grounds. Our chalet stands intact and dry amongst the wreckage of the campground. Ouma's prayers have worked. We stay.

Auntie Claudia and Uncle Teo, and their girls, vacation in Beira with us, too.

One year, I am older, around fifteen, perhaps. Before Christmas, we set off for Beira from Chiredzi to meet up with Auntie Claudia and Uncle Teo in Fort Vic. We will all travel together from there. The rains this year have been torrential, raining meerkats and porcupines for weeks on end.

The first stage of our journey in our car laden with kids, suitcases, *padkos*, and whatever else we can squeeze in takes us over the Tokwe River to the turnoff for Fort Vic. As we crest the hill just before the river, we come to a screeching halt. Cars and buses are lined up in front of the bridge. Some are pulled over onto the verge of the muddy road. A brown torrent rages downriver, and all we can see of the bridge are the tips of little posts on either side sticking up through the turbid water. Our hearts sink, and Dad shakes his head. "There's no way we'll be able to cross."

We groan. Some cars are turning around and heading back to where they have come from. At that moment, we notice a bus making its way slowly—ever so slowly—across the bridge, leaving behind it a churning wake. We hold our breaths. If the bus goes over, it will be tragic. It is packed to the gills with people. *Why do they even try?* I ask myself. We breathe a sigh of relief as it, at last, reaches the other side and crawls out of the water like a swamp thing, and groans up the hill. A cheer goes up. Another bus follows, then a car. The cars are not as heavy or large as the buses, so a group of African men who wait with us on our side of the river pile onto the hoods and trunks of each car to weigh them down. They escort a vehicle across, returning with a car from the other side and then helping the next vehicle cross. I can't believe what I am seeing. These men are risking their lives to assist the makiwa in getting to their destinations. There is no reason for them to do it. Still, typical of the Africans' cooperative spirit, they are willing to help others even when it is not in their own best interest.

It is now our turn. As our hearts skip beats, the men jump on our car, back and front. Dad cautiously approaches the bridge, and our front wheels hit the water. We feel a slight jolt. My hands are sweaty, and no one breathes. We begin to creep across the bridge, looking at the dirty copper-tinged flux we are defying. It is even more frightening than what we have observed from the river bank. Large branches, carried by the force of the water, shoot past our bow. Our car feels light — too light. It seems to float, but still, we creep forward. As laden as we are, we have no idea if we will be lucky or not. No one has gone over yet, but every now and then, we feel the car lift slightly, then its tires settle back onto the bridge surface, and we continue. *What if we stall? What if...* I can't finish my thought. The roar of the water drowns out any other sound, not that anyone is saying anything. We all sit, numb with terror as the car inches across the wide river. Time seems to hang suspended, but finally, we reach the other side, and our tires meet the solid ground again. With cheers, lots of handshaking, and our thanks to the brave men, we proceed.

Although the sensible thing may have been to turn around and go home, this is Africa, and we do things differently here. I am only thankful we and the others who cross this day survive.

This Christmas is worth braving the river. Instead of a chalet at the Estoril, we rent a house in Beira. It isn't near the beach, but it possesses a considerable yard punctuated by shady cashew trees. We enjoy the camaraderie of friends our age, staying up past our bedtime and sneaking to the kitchen for midnight snacks of green olives and cheese.

I am fascinated by the cashew trees. Hanging from clusters of large, shiny green leaves are brilliant, pear-shaped red "apples." Under each apple, a nut in a hard, brown shell curves down. I do not know, though, that the cashew is not really a nut; it is a seed. Neither do I know that the nut, or seed, must be chemically treated before it becomes edible. The cashew is related to poison ivy and has a toxic sap that protects it. I decide, as if picking walnuts, that I will eat a nut straight from the tree. I imagine bragging to my friends how I had sat under a real cashew tree eating real cashew nuts. We have only seen cashews in jars, and I will be one of the few in my circle who has seen an actual cashew tree. From a lower branch, I pluck an "apple," separating the seed from the fruit, and eagerly tear off the nut's outer shell. I pop the soft, pale yellow seed into my mouth.

I scream. My mouth is on fire! I spit the seed out and sprint inside to find some water, drinking it by the liter, but it doesn't help. For days after that, my mouth and lips are red and swollen. I learn about eating raw cashews the hard way.

I am not the only fool. Growing in the same garden are bushes with pretty red fruits. Butch and Rabbit find the siren song of nature's beauty irresistible, much like me with the cashews, and harvest handfuls of the pods. It is not long before we are alerted to screams from the back yard. Butch and Rabbit are sitting on the ground near their haul of piri-piri pods, eyes streaming and faces glowing red. Small heaps of piri-piri pods abandoned on the ground tell us the story. They have rubbed their eyes with hands contaminated with the volatile oils from the chili pods, and the more it burns, the more they rub their eyes. It takes Mom and Dad the whole day to repeatedly wash their eyes out with water, which doesn't work, so they revert to milk, which does finally seem to work.

Despite the storms, flooded rivers, toxic nuts, the chili-eye wash, and the pesky men on the beach, we love our Beira vacations and return again and again. I imagine I am on another continent, that I am sitting on a beach in Spain or Portugal, or walking down a cobbled street in Madrid, or sitting at a sidewalk café in Lisbon. Africa feels very far away.

CHAPTER 47

HOME SCHOOLING

1965-1966

In 1965 in the US, riots, blackouts, and the Vietnam War rage while in Rhodesia, our Prime Minister Ian Smith declares unilateral independence from Britain. Little do I know, since I am still only fourteen, that this political event ensures that the Bush War, which began last year in our country, will not only continue, but escalate. Right now, I am a self-absorbed teen, and war, or politics, is barely perceptible in my life. My only concerns are school and making friends.

My report card, compliments of the not-yet-retired Mr. Tenenbaum, is disappointing. It states, "...Reads too many comics." It is true, but not the whole story. I also draw comics and have my own school magazine in comic form that comes out weekly. It skewers our teachers with lame school-girl humor, but it is immensely popular, and even some teachers are eager to get the next copy. They enjoy being a feature topic.

I am still good at some subjects, such as art, English, geography, and history, but fail miserably in math. Algebra may as well be taught in Korean for all I understand of it. I am equally bad at science. My friend Angela and I pass notes, giggle, throw spitballs, and act up in science. Our teacher ejects us both from the class regularly, so I don't get to absorb much.

My sojourn at the church school is ending soon. Their curriculum does not extend into the final years of high school. Mom and Dad have decided that, after 1966, none of their children will return to this school.

Belatedly, Mom is shocked to hear from us that our now erstwhile principal, Mr. Tenenbaum, who has since retired, burned all library books not religious in nature, and the stench of scandal from his successor still lingers in their nostrils. I am flabbergasted that it has taken them so long to realize our education is not the best, either. They choose not to pull us out immediately, though, and we will complete our school year here with a new principal, one of our teachers. Rabbit will attend boarding school in Fort Vic. Butch talks them into sending her to our church's high school in South Africa. Queenie is already attending day school in Chiredzi.

What to do with Pie, they must ponder in their bedroom one hot night, Dad, no doubt eating peanuts under the mosquito netting as he reads a Zane Gray western while Mom sneaks a chocolate *bon-bon* she has saved from the zombie chocoholic horde. I can only imagine how the conversation goes.

"She wants to go to this school, in America, no less," Mom says, handing an open magazine to Dad. The Tilly lamp casts a golden glow on the glossy magazine. "Look at this ad."

Dad snorts. "What the hell is this? A pipedream. Will never happen," he shakes his head.

Katlynn Brooke

"I know, but what will we do with her? It *is* a religious school." Mom is always a sucker for religion.

"It looks expensive. Where does she get this magazine from?"

"It's a church magazine. They have this school in Pasadena, California."

"Over my dead body."

"Mine too. I'll home school her, again."

And that is pretty much that. I will stay at home and complete my final years under Mom's tutelage. She enrolls me in the government-run correspondence school. At the start of 1966, I will complete my "O" Levels (GED equivalent) under her tutelage. Since Rhodesia is under the British educational system, we follow British schools' curriculum. "O" Levels are the minimum standard needed to graduate high school. There are two others, "M" Level and "A" Level, which can guarantee a university's continuing education. Thanks to my lackadaisical education, I do not possess the required courses to enter this curriculum. I am doomed to be a worker bee rather than an academic or professional.

I am broken-hearted, but once again, I have no choice. I resign myself to spending my final school years at home, but that will not begin until next year.

Our rough living is almost over, though. The canals are finishing up, and Dad's construction company has jobs for him in Chiredzi. Meanwhile, we still suffer bush living as we complete our stint at the boarding school. However, there are some bright spots and still more care-free school vacations ahead.

CHAPTER 48

THE DUCHESS

M om has made some friends, and it gives us comfort that at least one of them lives much as we do.

I will call her the Duchess—an Afrikaner lady with a camp situated not too far from ours. While home on school vacation, I enjoy visiting with the Duchess. Her camp, by comparison to ours, is luxurious and reminds me of a Viking longhouse. The Duchess never visits our camp, and I don't blame her. Our homestead is caveman living at best.

Her living and dining room is a large, airy, rectangular structure built from sturdy upright timbers and mud-plastered walls. There are no patches or gaping holes like our mud and straw-built dining room. The pitched thatch roof, with massive log beams, allows for a comfortable temperature. The Duchess' freshly upholstered teak furniture with bright, stuffed cushions makes me want to sink down into them and pretend it is my home. I take deep breaths of the freshly circulating air that smells of dry grass and floor polish. The floors are impeccably clean, swept clear of all dirt, and polished to a high gloss with paraffin wax.

The Duchess is as carefully put-together as her home and belongings. No bare feet enter this dwelling. Her stiletto heels click-clack on the concrete floor as she leads us into her abode.

Tea, Scones, and Malaria

"Kom in, kom in — come in," she beckons, her perfectly manicured, glossy red fingernails curved like talons. In her fifties, the Duchess' coifed hair is hennaed to an inch of its life, reminding me of a clown. Heavy, penciled-in eyebrows top violent blue eyeshadow from lid to brow and mascara-slathered false eyelashes that look like hairy spiders. I wonder if her mirror shows her the same thing I am seeing.

The circus effect stops at her neck, but below that, it is Christmas. Baubles and beads decorate her neck, wrists, ears, and fingers. Everywhere one looks, where skin shows, is a glittering object or a ceramic bead, like a gypsy fortune-teller at a country carnival. Nothing matches; everything jangles and jingles, and I love it.

The Duchess rings a small brass bell, her bracelets tinkling, and the houseman, wearing a white uniform with a red fez on his head, magically appears from the kitchen.

"Tea for the madams, Egbert," the Duchess orders, "And a plate of scones, with cream and jam." Egbert silently disappears. At home, we usually just yell, "Tea!" and Petina, if she feels like it, will make it happen. The tea arrives quickly, along with a porcelain plate piled high with scones and small bowls of jam and cream. The Duchess pours a small amount of cream into each teacup, then, once the tea has steeped, she places a small tea sieve on a cup and fills the cup with a rich, red-brown brew. "One lump, or two?" She asks, poising the silver tongs over the china sugar bowl.

We sip from delicate porcelain cups; an ornate flower-decorated, gold-trimmed tea-set, requiring one to lift one's pinkie finger. Everything matches. As the Duchess sips, her lipstick leaves a perfect red stencil of her lips on the rim of her cup.

I am a robot on an assembly line, my hand moving from the plate of scones to my mouth. I eat as if I have never seen food before, and Mom blushes.

"I think you've had enough, don't you?"

"*Ag man*, let her have some more. She's all skin and bones," the Duchess says, and I smile at her gratefully as I grab another scone. The Duchess winks at me, so for good measure, I take another scone.

It is depressing to return to our colorless campsite and sit on our scratched, faded chairs at a table that looks like it has been used by a pride of lions to sharpen their claws. We drink out of mismatched cups. We eat off of discolored plastic dinnerware that has long ago waved the white flag and now longs for a decent burial. It warms my heart to know that bush life does not need to destroy one's pride, that there is still someone who, faced with the same hardships as us, does not allow circumstances to pour cold water on her dignity. While her appearance seems ridiculous to me, it also makes me understand that this lady will not be cowed by rough bush living. She keeps her spirits and personal pride up and does it with much aplomb.

Dad informs us we are moving closer to town, into another semi-permanent construction, a Quonset hut. I am beginning to feel our bush days are nearly over. *Will I miss our camp life?* I wonder. I am uncertain.

Tea, Scones, and Malaria

CHAPTER 49

AMANDA AND INGA

1966

This year is the dawning of the Cultural Revolution of Mao Tse Tung in China, and in Rhodesia, petrol rationing begins, making travel a little more difficult for us. We are beginning to feel the effects of world economic sanctions levied against our illegal government, and the Bush War is heating up. I hear on the radio that our government is considered "illegal" because, in 1965, our Prime Minister Ian Smith declared UDI, a universal declaration of independence by the white minority government, without the approval of Britain. We broke away from the Commonwealth and are now an independent rogue country. I am still not terribly concerned, though, and my perspective on life is optimistic. We don't see beyond our noses.

On the home front, while no permanent home is yet available for us, we move closer to town and into a Quonset hut with some well-constructed add-ons in the vein of the Duchess's camp. We still use the caravan, and that becomes my bedroom. I am now fifteen, old enough not to be forced to share a room with my siblings. This home has some comforts, such as electricity and running water, and more neighbors.

Our closest neighbors are an English family, the Hills. I befriend their daughter, Amanda, who is my age, and her younger brother, Matthew. Although the Hills are English, and Amanda was born in London, her family moved to Scotland when she was still young, so she speaks with a slight Scottish accent. Matthew, however, was born in Scotland, and he only speaks Gaelic. Or he speaks English that sounds like Gaelic. I am never sure which it is.

"How do you understand him?" I ask Amanda.

"I don't. Not even my parents understand him."

"Why is he following us?"

"He doesn't have anyone else to talk to."

So, we tolerate him and ignore his incomprehensible chatter. He enjoys being our shadow. We go for walks in the bush, and Matthew trails behind, talking non-stop. While we discuss which pop stars we prefer—Cliff Richard, Engelbert Humperdinck, Roy Orbison, or Elvis—Matthew prattles on and on behind us.

"In Scotland I was a 'Mod,'" Amanda proudly proclaims, ignoring her brother.

"What's that?"

"We have the 'Mods' and the 'Rockers'," she explains. I belong to the Mods. We aren't much like the Rockers, although they're always looking to fight with us. They wear leather jackets and slick back their hair. They also ride motorcycles."

I nod. So that is why Amanda loves Roy Orbison. He is more in keeping with the Mod's clean-cut image, while the Rockers are Elvis fans. I realize with a start that Dustin, the ducktail Dad had so hated back in 1958, is definitely a Rocker. According to Amanda, the Rockers are the ones who are always in trouble with the law. She is proud to be a Mod, and I wish I lived in London so I can be one, too. I doubt there are any Mods or Rockers in Rhodesia, let alone our neck of the bush.

The Beatles, by this time, have performed their last concert. I am grief-stricken. I wear my hair in the classic "mop-top" for which they are so famous. I have never been to a Beatles concert, and I never will, but my room is plastered with Beatles posters. My favorite is George. I think he is the best-looking. I don't care if he is considered by my peers not to be the best musically.

Unfortunately, Amanda's family does not stay long in Chiredzi. I am not sure where they go to, but we get new neighbors; John, an Englishman, with his Norwegian wife Inga, and their two small children, Edward and Anne. I miss Amanda terribly, but I quickly befriend Inga. She is young, blonde, and beautiful. She looks like a model and is a hairdresser by trade.

Everyone admires Inga. I feel proud to know she is also my neighbor and friend. I spend many hours at her house and am her main baby-sitter. Her two children, Edward and Anne, are eight and five, and I adore them. Inga, like Mom, treats her children like little adults. There is no baby talk; the children speak in well-formed, complete sentences. But our friendship doesn't last. John and Inga leave Chiredzi to return to Europe, and as for us, we are moving again.

CHAPTER 50

SNAKES AND JERRYMUNGLUMS

It is 1966, and Butch is in school in Cape Town, Rabbit is a boarder at Fort Vic high school, while Queenie attends the Chiredzi junior school. I am now being home schooled in my final year of high school. Dad has left the construction company and works for the sugar estates, at the sugar mill, and we have been supplied with other lodgings in Hippo Valley: three Quonset huts joined together to make something that looks cozy and comfortable. It is bigger and has less of a "camping" feel than the place we have just left. It is the closest thing to a house we've had in a long time. We have electricity, indoor plumbing, and potable running water. The best feature of this home is that we are less than a mile from the country club. Across from the house and wide main dirt road, the sugar fields stretch to the horizon, our house, the mill, the club, and residential area islands in a sea of green. Our house is sandwiched between these fields and two sugar mills.

Not long after moving here, I awaken to make a bathroom call. I usually get out of bed on the left, because my bedroom door is on the left, but this night I turn on the light next to my bed, sleepily roll out on the right, and stumble toward the door. I glance down, and exactly where I would place my feet, a black snake lies coiled up next to my bed, its forked tongue flicking in and out of its mouth.

I run to my parent's bedroom. There's a tremor in my voice as I shake Dad awake. "There's a snake under my bed." He snorts, rolls over, squinting at me. Mom stirs and gives a slight moan as she settles back into sleep, snoring softly.

"A snake?" Dad goes from fast asleep to fully awake in a nano-second, leaping out of bed, snatching his always handy rifle, and running ahead of me to my bedroom, one of the Quonset huts in our new home.

Dad pushes the bolt on the rifle, then lifts it to aim. The snake has not moved. It still lies there as if it is a welcome guest instead of a terrifying interloper. With a sigh and a shake of his head, Dad places the rifle down. He bends over and pinches the snake behind its head, the inky body twisting in his grip.

"It's only a mole snake. You woke me up for this...," he shakes his head. "They keep the rats out, and they're not poisonous. You should have seen that for yourself."

It is true. Dad has taught us about snakes: which are poisonous, which are not, and how to tell them apart. If I'd taken the time to really observe, I would have identified it as a mole snake. Still, I would not have been able to dispatch it. That, I think, is Dad's job, but he seems to think I should have spent the rest of the night with the snake. "It will leave on its own before morning," he explains, as if it is only a man-snake on a booty call. He opens the front door and tosses the writhing critter out into the night, back to the cane fields where it belongs, then goes back to bed. I don't sleep for the rest of the night. If I'd placed my feet on top of the snake, it surely would have bitten me, and I would be the one to have the heart-attack. Providence kept me from getting out of bed that night on the wrong side.

In the cane fields, snakes aren't our only concern. The rainy season brings bugs out of their winter hiding places like teens converging on a Rolling Stones concert. One species is the critter known as a Jerrymunglum. I am not alone in my terror of these critters that are so pervasive when the rains begin. No one knows where the name Jerrymunglum comes from, but I am sure it originates from someone with a sense of humor. They are also known as Romans, rain spiders, or camel spiders. Technically, they are not true spiders, but no one can ever convince me of this. It looks like a spider, but it has ten legs instead of eight. Two of the "legs" are palps, feelers that are used to navigate their way around. They grow to enormous sizes, up to five inches, and they run like the wind, also inspiring another name: wind spider. What makes these creatures extra fearsome is that they have a tendency to run directly toward any screaming human trying to escape, usually me.

"They try to get into your shadow," Dad informs us. "They're not trying to attack you." But this factoid does not convince us. A screaming Ouma once jumped into the bathtub to get away from one, and it followed her into the tub. I have never seen my grandmother move so fast. We find this amusing. Munglums are not toxic, though, and despite their large jaws, seldom bite.

I sit in my bed at night, with the light on and a shoe nearby, my eyes peeled for movement. When I see one, I pick up the shoe, hurling it at the shadow that flits across the floor.

Most of the time, I miss. I yell out for Dad to come and kill the spider, but he is not amused.

"They won't bite you," he grumbles as he hunts down and dispatches the intruder with my shoe. "They're harmless. How can I sleep if you're always calling me to kill something?"

How can *I* sleep, I mutter back, but Dad remains unmoved. Snakes, spiders, and creepy-crawlies bother him not a whit.

There are some insects, though, that I do not fear. *Chongololos*, dark brown millipedes with a hard exoskeleton outer shell, their many legs all seeming to work in concert without tripping up, are our favorite. We are fascinated by them. When we disturb a chongololo—as we often do, by poking it with a stick—it curls up into a tight ball, all its legs tucked inside. It is now safe to pick up these small balls and let them sit in our hand for a while before releasing them, unmolested, to continue their merry way. A threatened millipede squirts the attacker with an odorous substance that can be corrosive. The African name chongololo means to roll up. We think it funny, allowing the syllables to slowly and deliciously roll off our tongues: *"Chong...go...lo...lo!"*

While we're in walking distance to the club, and our new home is an improvement on the camps, our close proximity to the cane fields ensures a variety of snake and insect life that I never quite get used to.

CHAPTER 51

COUNTRY CLUB LIFE

Sugar Mill, Hippo Valley Estates

We are only about a ten or fifteen-minute drive to Chiredzi. The country club run by the sugar estates becomes our new backyard, our playground, and our social life suddenly seems much brighter. Dad, in particular, finds the club a godsend. He takes up golf, and it quickly becomes an obsession.

On one of our visits to South Africa, Dad receives a bag of second-hand golf clubs from his brother, a gift from one of his golf buddies, Gary Player. Although this is not known to us at the time, Player is Dad's sixth cousin on his mother's side. Dad is honored and delighted to have a set of the famous golfer's clubs.

"It will be a sin not to use Gary Player's clubs," he says.

Suddenly, there is trouble in paradise.

"I'm a golf widow," Mom complains to everyone within earshot. "I don't see him anymore. He's always at the club on the weekends, golfing with his pals. I want him to make furniture for us—I'm tired of this old stuff we've dragged with us from pillar to post, camp to camp, over the years. He promised me he'd make a new dining room table with chairs..." Dad's promises are sincere, but he is now a golf-a-holic—his nine holes turn into eighteen, and before he knows it, the sun is setting behind the clubhouse.

"I've been asked to have dinner with the guys," he'll say as he runs into the house for a quick shower and change of clothing. "We're celebrating Tom's first birdie on hole eight..." or "I've been asked to advise the committee on redesigning the clubhouse... don't expect me home until late."

"He's never cheated on me with women," Mom comments with a sigh, "but I never expected I'd be competing with a driving masher, niblick, or putter. I don't stand a chance."

We all make use of the swimming pool, tennis courts, and outdoor movie theater. The club has movies every Friday night, with chairs arranged on the big lawn. We bring our supper or snacks in Tupperware containers or order food and drinks from the snack bar. Black and white serial films from the '30s and '40s are our usual fare, along with old movie-tone newsreels. Once a week, relatively recent feature movies are flown in.

"Don't ask me to go to a movie unless it's a western," Dad informs us. "I'll go if it's John Wayne. I don't want to waste my time on those idiotic musicals you all love so much. I hate them!"

"But...but Dad, we need you there," we say. Mom can drive us to the club—heck, we can walk—but it's comforting to be there with both our parents, and most importantly, Dad is easier to persuade to shell out for snacks at the snack bar. Mom's penny-pinching ways may be behind our mercenary desire for Dad's presence. He refuses, frequently, and we are forced to take our own snacks, whatever we can find in the house, which usually isn't much.

One night an Elvis musical, *Blue Hawaii*, is showing at the club. Except for Dad and Rabbit, we want to see this movie, and we want Dad to go with us. Rabbit can take it or leave it. He takes it. We know there is nothing in the house worth noshing on, though, and the snack bar is calling us.

"We'll tell him it's a John Wayne movie," Mom suggests. She is as devious as we are. We laugh and keep our devil's bargain.

When we arrive at the club, we cajole some coins out of Dad, quickly buying our burgers and chips at the snack bar before the film begins to roll. The opening credits appear on the screen, a large Paramount Pictures logo superimposed over Diamond Head. *Night and you and blue Hawaii...* The mellow voice of Presley washes over us like a wave on

Waikiki Beach and we sigh and sink back into our plastic chairs.

Dad moans, "Oh no! Elvis Presley!" Grumbling under his breath and shooting us a death-stare, he rises. Simultaneously, our neighbor, sitting with his wife and daughters in the row in front of us, stands up, shaking his head and mumbling something unprintable.

The neighbor's wife turns to Mom, laughing. "I told him it was a war movie."

More often than not, though, the movie projector breaks down in the middle of the movie or even before it begins. A collective groan goes up as the burn expands out across the screen like a spreading cancer; the clackity-clack of the film strip informing us we won't be watching any more movies this evening. Sometimes the problem isn't too serious; a bulb burns out, and it can be quickly fixed, but other times we need to wait days for a part to arrive. It often rains, and we drag our chairs inside to the auditorium and set everything up again. We are used to glitches—they have always been a part of our lives, and we develop a sense of humor about them.

The club is our oasis. It is the heartbeat of the Lowveld social scene, a bustling center of recreational activity with its movies, amateur concerts, pool, golf course, tennis courts, and dining room/bar. Everyone we know goes there, and we spend many evenings and weekends here. It is truly a delight.

CHAPTER 52

RABBIT

After a few months, we move again, but like the TV show *The Jeffersons*, we are "moving on up." This time, it is to a house not far from our Quonset house and even closer to the clubhouse. A three-bedroom, ranch-style home has become available. Petina "ah-ah's," a big grin on her face as we inspect the premises. She has stuck with us through the hard times, with barely tolerable quarters, and now she once again has good living and working conditions. Her son, Johnny, is a four-year-old and no longer living in a wheelbarrow.

Flamboyant trees with their scarlet flowers, purple jacarandas, and tropical plants such as the broad-leafed elephant ear, frond-like cycads, and pink bauhinias flourish in the sizable garden. A sturdy mulberry tree grows next to the house. We climb the tree and sate ourselves with ripe mulberries, our hands and feet staining purple. We gather leaves from the tree for our silkworms. We have shoe boxes filled with silkworms, and we watch, fascinated, as they munch unceasingly on the leaves. The unexceptional grayish-white moth that finally emerges belies the beautiful golden cocoons they spin. We collect the cocoons but have no idea what to do with them.

Mom and Dad are no longer teetotalers. They have drifted from the church's strict, no-drinking tenet and have discovered that drinking is a requirement in the Lowveld. Mom will have a small glass of sherry in the evenings, and Dad, the occasional beer with his golfing friends. Memories of their own fathers, though, are still too fresh in their minds for any over-imbibing.

One of Mom's friends has given her a recipe for making mulberry wine from our bumper crop. It is all the rage in the Lowveld to make your own wine. Perhaps, Mom tells us, it will make excellent table wine, cooking wine, or something she can give out as gifts to friends. She is optimistic about the outcome. More than she should have been. She prepares the sugar and water base, adds the mulberries and some raisins, and then the yeast and pectic acid. The final product is poured into large bottles that she leaves to age in the cabinet under the kitchen sink. She has been told that it is supposed to taste like a red wine if one allows it to ferment long enough; perhaps, about two years.

Not long after the fermentation process begins, Mom asks Butch, Queenie, and I to go shopping with her in Chiredzi. Rabbit does not want to go, so we leave him alone at home. He is no fun, anyway. We think he'll probably go ride his bike with Colin, the boy next door. They are both about age thirteen and often hang out together. We do our shopping, which takes a couple of hours, then make our way home.

I head into the house first with an armload of groceries and almost fall over something near the doorway. I look down. Rabbit is stretched out on the kitchen floor.

"Mom! Something's wrong with Rabbit!" He is ashen-faced and only semi-conscious, his eyes rolling up in his head.

We notice the empty glass clutched in his hand, and the open cabinet door under the sink tells us the story. The large wine-fermentation bottle, while not empty, is far from full. It takes us several hours to sober Rabbit up. We are fearful that he has been poisoned, but he does recover after vomiting up a purple swill. Mom samples the liquor and says it's too potent, more like brandy than wine, so she pours it down the sink and never attempts to make mulberry wine again.

This is not Rabbit's only brush with danger.

Home from the holidays, he is next door, riding his bike with Colin. I am outside in the garden when I notice Rabbit hobbling into the yard, clutching his stomach. "What happened?" I ask.

"I-I fell off my bike. The handlebars caught me in my stomach."

"Go lie down. Maybe you'll feel better later."

But he does not. When we check on him again, he is pale — even yellow. His breathing is shallow, and he is in obvious pain.

"We need to take him to the hospital," Mom says, and we help him into the car. He moans all the way to the small hospital that, thank God, we now have. It's not busy, and the doctor sees him right away. He calls Mom in after examining Rabbit.

"He needs emergency surgery," he tells her. "His liver has ruptured, and he has internal bleeding."

Tea, Scones, and Malaria

We call Dad off the golf course. We wait and wait, sitting nervously in the hospital waiting room. We pray. Dad's face is white, and Mom tries not to cry. The surgery seems to take hours, but finally, the doctor emerges. "He's stable, but I can't promise he'll make it," he tells us. "Go home," the doctor says, "there's nothing more anyone can do but wait."

We don't expect Rabbit to make it through the night. No one does. The prognosis is bleak. But this is the doctor who saved a man who once, not too long ago, had been trampled by an elephant. He, too, needed emergency surgery, and it is this same doctor who saved his life. I keep this in my thoughts throughout a sleepless night. First thing in the morning, we arrive back at the hospital.

"He'll make it," the doctor says, now a glint of hope in his eye. "But it will be a long recovery."

It is. For months, Rabbit is sickly and weak, his color jaundice yellow. He wastes away to almost nothing, but he survives. Once again, we are lucky.

CHAPTER 53

THE DANCE

I am lonely. I am now in my final year of high school, and I am not enjoying being home schooled. Looking back with 20/20 vision, I realize my parents couldn't afford to send three of us to boarding schools. They are barely scraping by as it is.

Two girls my age live next door—Kathy and Jeanne. When they are home, we do everything together, but during the school term, every teen in Hippo Valley and the Lowveld anywhere near my age is at boarding school. I suffer bouts of depression that nearly cripple me, and I long for the company of kids my own age. I go to the club pool to swim in the afternoons, but I am alone, aside from a few mothers with toddlers. I sit by myself and try not to cry. I join Dad for drinks at sundown, drinking Coke while he and his friends drink beer shandies, a popular Rhodesian drink of beer mixed with lemonade. I am tolerated in these groups, and I sit there nursing my Coke while Dad and his buddies crack silly jokes, gossip, and act as if I'm not there. These men are Dad's age, and even the younger ones are way too old for me.

Mom teaches me to type. She can quickly pound out over one hundred words a minute on a manual typewriter. She rarely makes a mistake. For me, it begins as the hunt and peck method, trying not to break my carefully manicured fingernails. Eventually, something clicks, and I begin to type faster on the old manual, although my accuracy is still in question. I thank Mom now for teaching me this skill. It has served me better than any other high school class I've taken, except perhaps English. With my love of reading, my aptitude for the English language, my writing skill, and the manual typewriter, I have all the author's tools at my disposal. However, I don't do a thing with the time I have to express myself on paper. Instead, I mope, feel sorry for myself, and try to figure out ways to get out of the house. In other words, I am a typical teen.

I am surprised Mom never kills me.

I discover sarcasm and acidity, and I quickly learn how to weaponize them. One day, my gentle mother rises from the table, draws back her hand, and delivers a stinging slap to my face. She has never hit me before. She has never even raised her voice. She remembers how she was treated by her father, and she does not want to behave that way to her own children, but I have overstepped even her fluid boundaries. She has become her father.

I don't know who is more shocked — her or me. We stare at each other for a moment before we both begin to cry. This episode makes me realize Mom does have boundaries, and we treat each other more respectfully from that moment on. Mom is my friend. Child-rearing experts say it is not advisable to be your child's friend, but Mom pays that no mind. She treats me as an equal.

On the other hand, Dad is the enforcer, and I live in fear of him. Dad is pleased I have no friends, especially boyfriends. He keeps me on a short leash, and we frequently come to loggerheads over his restrictive rules.

He is not this way toward his other children. Butch, and later Rabbit, and Queenie, can do pretty much as they please. He sets rules for his eldest that are more applicable to the Victorian era. Mom and I ponder this, and we never learn why Dad is stricter with me than with his other children. I understand only much later that he sees a vulnerability in me he doesn't see in his other children. He is over-protective, and it does not serve me well in my life. I have no opportunity to expand emotionally or to learn how to cope with relationships. I become stunted.

One night, the club has a dance, and I want to go since Kathy and Jeanne are home from school and are going with some boys our age.

"Over my dead body," Dad says, his stock response to anything I want.

I am stunned at his adamant refusal, but Mom intervenes on my behalf.

"Well, only if you're home by 11 p.m.," Dad relents. I promise. I would have pledged on a Bible to cut off my arm with a rusty saw if that had been a condition, but I do have every intention of keeping my promise.

I enjoy the evening even more than I can imagine. I meet a young man named Ian, and we dance to Chubby Checker, the Beatles, the Stones, and Jefferson Airplane. We do The Twist, then the music changes to slow dancing and, for the first time in my life, I am in close physical contact with a male.

I like the feeling and I rarely sit down. Like Eliza Doolittle in *My Fair Lady*, I could have danced all night. Everyone is at the dance—all the kids my age, along with many adults. The auditorium is crowded, and the party atmosphere makes me feel that I am no longer alone and isolated. I am so immersed in the music and my partner it takes me some time to register what is happening behind me.

The crowd parts as a man, clad in bathrobe and slippers, makes his way across the dance floor, elbowing people out of the way. I gape, along with everyone else, and then, to my utter humiliation and shame, I realize the man is Dad. He grabs me by my elbow, glaring at Ian.

"It's midnight!" he yells over the loud music. "I told you to be home by eleven! I sat outside honking for you. Didn't you hear me?"

How could I? The music is jet airplane decibel level. I couldn't have heard a nearby volcanic eruption. I want the roof to cave in on me, but the building remains stubbornly stable. Not even a small tremor or any distraction that will turn the one hundred or so pairs of eyes now on me away. My friends gawk at me, horror and pity in their eyes, as Dad drags me to the exit. Ian slinks away, merging into the crowd as if he has no idea who the girl is that he has been dancing with all night.

Dad shouts at me all the way home. I crawl into bed, not even bothering to undress, and sob myself to sleep.

No one mentions the episode. Kathy and Jeanne act as if it never happened. I don't know if this is a good thing or a bad thing. To my immense surprise, Ian returns and wants to date me. I had given him my address before Dad showed up. However, I discover I don't really like him. Dad doesn't seem to mind Ian; now that he gets to know him, I think he gives Ian points for being brave enough to face him. We never break the check-in time again, though. He always brings me back before my curfew is up. Much to my own relief, Ian and I don't really hit it off, and he quickly disappears into the blue yonder.

Dad's jealousy and strictness are not over, though. He always keeps me on his radar, wanting to know where I am and who is with me. He is right to do so, but at the time, I do not appreciate it. Not one bit.

Tea, Scones, and Malaria

CHAPTER 54

A TRAIN AND A HOLE-IN-ONE

Old Consul left. Mom, Pie (holding cat), Butch in tree

1967

In 1967 Dr. Christiaan Barnard carries out the first heart transplant in Groote Schuur Hospital, Cape Town.

"I've met him," Mom says as we devour all the details in the newspaper about the transplant. "Back in the forties. My best friend in college was once engaged to him." The engagement didn't last, though, and Dr. Barnard moved on, but we are proud that this pioneering doctor is a South

African. Many years later, I discover that he, too, is a remote cousin on Mom's side of the family. We share a common ancestor from the 1700s, as many South Africans do.

Dad is forty-five years old when he has his first heart attack — on the golf course. He insists upon finishing his game first before going to the hospital. He survives the heart attack and returns to the game as quickly as he can. Not long after that, he is reaching for his ball in the rough. Hidden by the long grass, he does not see the snake that bites him. His buddies urge him to go to the hospital, but Dad turns a deaf ear to their pleas.

"If I can't identify the snake that bit me, what good will it do me to go to the hospital? They won't know what anti-venom to give me." He has a point. He continues with his game. He tells us later that he will rather die playing golf than waiting at the hospital to die. No doubt it helps to be a golfer to understand his choice. His hand swells up, it hurts a bit, but other than that, he is none the worse for the bite.

The highlight of Dad's life comes not at our weddings, not at Mom's success in selling paintings, not at any of his kid's graduations, but the day he gets a hole-in-one. That day, Mom and us kids are returning from Bulawayo in her old Consul, now a decrepit pile of nuts and bolts held together by a wish and a prayer. We jounce over the rutted, corrugated dirt road toward Chiredzi, hoping the car won't disintegrate before we reach home. Somewhere between Chiredzi and Triangle, our nearest town, we must cross a railway line. There is no barrier across the road, but we can see a train approaching along the track as we near the crossing that is on a rise. Mom hits the brakes. Nothing happens. We continue to rattle along. She stands on the brake pedal — still nothing. We are flying now, clouds of dust billowing behind us. She screams. We scream. We stiffen, hands to mouth. No one knows what to do.

Mom applies the hand brake, but the car doesn't slow. She tries throwing the car into a lower gear, but the gears only grind ominously, and our trajectory toward the crossing continues. The train is drawing nearer, and so are we. It is now only a matter of who is going to reach the crossing first. The train driver leans on his air horn — it blares in our ears like a rogue elephant on the rampage. The train driver has undoubtedly seen the terrible accident that is about to occur, but there is nothing he can do.

We hit the rails, and the car lifts, going airborne as it crests the rise. We bounce back onto the road on the other side just as the engine roars behind us, horn still bellowing. The train has missed us by inches. Eventually, we trundle to a halt on the side of the road.

Pale and shaking, we tumble out of the car, hugging each other in relief that we're not dead. It doesn't take long before a good Samaritan stops and picks us up, taking us to Hippo Valley and our home. We are all still traumatized as we walk into the house.

Minutes later, Dad comes home too, a big grin on his unusually flushed face.

"We were almost killed today!" Mom shouts before he can say anything. She begins to tell him the story about the brakes and the train when he interrupts.

"I got a hole-in-one!"

"We almost died!"

"They served us champagne at the clubhouse! I had to drink it out of a shoe!"

True, he seems a little tipsy. *Drunk*, perhaps? We stare at him in shock. Mom's slack jaw tells us she doesn't know what to say, either, but she tries.

"The car is still sitting on the road! We had to find a lift home!"

"I'm the first person in the Lowveld to get a hole-in-one!"

We escaped a gory death by inches, and all he can talk about is his golf game. When Dad sobers up, he apologizes, and we allow ourselves to celebrate with him. Not with alcohol, though.

We are proud that he has had a hole-in-one. His life has been so difficult from an early age that it affects how he makes decisions, treats us, and informs his beliefs. If we hadn't been so taken up with our own event of the day, we would have seen just how much he needed us then to validate his achievement and celebrate it with him.

CHAPTER 55

STRIP ROADS AND CONVOYS

Convoy

1968

In 1968 the assassination of Martin Luther King shocks the world. In Rhodesia, the Bush War to combat white rule is just beginning to heat up. In the Sixties, guerillas make incursions from Zambia to the north and attack outlying farms or villages. Travelers on the roads are vulnerable to land mines and roving bands of guerillas. Our army is small, so, to ensure the safety of civilians, and travelers, we have "Dad's Army."

Tea, Scones, and Malaria

Dad's Army is a rag-tag group of men, too old for service, who volunteer to guard travelers on the road. They form a convoy of vehicles interspersed with men on the back of Toyota bakkies wielding machine guns or any other weapon they can acquire.

The guerillas attack anything that looks vulnerable, and a lone traveler is extremely vulnerable. In 1968, the year I turn eighteen, we avoid the conflict by living in areas still considered safe. At this time, though, if we travel anywhere, we often do so by convoy. I do not hear of many problems in our area, and we still feel safe enough to live our lives normally. Guerillas and landmines are not the only hazard of travel, though.

If there is one thing Rhodesia may be famous for, it is its strip tar roads. Begun in the 1930s to save money, two asphalt strips were laid on a dirt road, an axle width apart. This parsimonious approach allows for more dirt roads to have at least some semblance of paving. Since only one vehicle can proceed at a time, when a car is encountered coming from the opposite direction, both vehicles move over to their respective sides of the road. Two wheels remain on one strip while the other two hit the dirt verge. It's a risky move, since having such disparate surfaces while traveling at speed means things often get tricky. It is easy to lose control and leave the road altogether, but every driver quickly learns how to navigate our bad roads.

In happier days, when we travel to the South African border, it is our family's custom to always stop at The Lion and the Elephant, a watering hole halfway between Beitbridge and the turnoff to Chiredzi. The hotel is an

Katlynn Brooke

African fantasy on the banks of a river plucked from the pages of a Hemmingway novel. The main building reminds us of our bush days, with a thatch roof, breezy verandah, and a river view. The rooms are individual rondavels—round, African style huts with thatch roofs—or rectangular bungalows. It is a treat to sit on the verandah and watch the sun set over the river. But during the Bush War, convoys of travelers on the strip road hurtle past it without stopping.

In more peaceful times, Dad is a good driver and he's used to navigating strip roads. Mom is not a reliable driver. Mom treats driving as if it is an afterthought. It seems as if she sometimes remembers that she is behind the wheel and needs to keep her focus on the road, otherwise her attention wanders. She admires the scenery, turns her head to talk to us, divests herself of an item of clothing such as her cardigan, all while speeding down the road. It may be, though, that this is an indicator that she is an exceptionally skilled driver, since she's never had an accident. She rarely takes her car in to be serviced or to have the oil changed. She never checks fluids and waits until it is running on fumes before filling up the tank. We frequently run out of gas at inopportune times, and her car is always breaking down somewhere alongside the road. Her brakes have failed more than once. The first time is when we almost hit the train, and the next time her brakes fail just as we approach an intersection. We plow into a sugar cane field, narrowly missing a truck coming from the other direction.

One day in 1968, we must join a convoy to the border in order to travel to South Africa to visit relatives. The convoy is waiting for travelers to arrive, and at the scheduled time, we pull out onto the Beitbridge road. One truck is in front, one in the middle, with another one bringing up the rear. Dad's Army, the men on the bakkies, keep their fingers on the triggers of their rifles, machine guns and other weapons. They speed down the strip tar road as if all the devils in hell are after us. It takes skilled driving to keep up, and we are aware that laggers are left behind. No one stops since it puts the whole column at risk. The rear truck may just go around you, and all you will see is a cloud of dust as the convoy speeds away.

Dad will not allow Mom to drive in a convoy. He always insists upon driving. This is fine in normal times, but this year, after several heart attacks, Dad is on heavy-duty medication, which makes him loopy. He doesn't inform us what kind of drug it is, but we think it is something for his "nerves," since he is under constant stress. Although they are not drinkers, Mom and Dad both rely heavily upon their pills, such as Valium, or something else in that category. Doctors prescribe them like breath mints, and they are easy to come by.

Hitting the strip road at sixty or seventy mph while under the influence of an opiate is not a laughing matter, and on this day, we aren't laughing.

"Let me drive," Mom insists. We look at each other. Dad is weaving all over the road. Perhaps Mom is the better choice, but we're not sure.

"I'm fine," Dad grunts. His knuckles are white as he grips the wheel, and his face is pale. Once or twice, the convoy pulls over—something they never do—to ask Dad if he is alright. He declares, in an outraged tone, that of course he is alright. We proceed, and Mom begs him to get out from behind the wheel so she can take over. He still refuses. His foot remains stubbornly on the gas pedal as we hit sixty mph. Sixty is not high speed on a good highway, but on a strip road it can be suicidal. The convoy is doing at least this, and we must keep up, but at what cost? We are terrified, and angry with Dad. His eyes are at half-mast, and he seems to be nodding off. Sometimes our wheels leave the strip with a thunk! He over-corrects, and the wheels leave the strip again with another thunk! on the other side.

As our convoy hurtles down the road, I miss our peace-time trips, when we would sing songs, play games such as "I Spy" or have a contest to see who can spot an animal that is not a cow or goat. Butch and I firmly believe that when we spot a white horse, the next male we observe will be our future husband. We vie to see who can be the first to spot a white horse. It doesn't matter to us that the first male we see is always Rabbit or Dad. Throughout the Bush War, though, we keep our eyes on the road and ignore the empty bush flashing by. Now we surveil the strip road for landmines.

Well-placed landmines are difficult to spot, but there can be tell-tale signs, such as a piece of trash that might mark the location of a mine, or a disturbance in the sandy verge, as if the ground has recently been dug up. We've heard of travelers who encounter these mines in a vehicle, and often the guerillas lurk nearby to finish off any survivors. On this trip I wonder what will come first for us—a sudden encounter with a baobab tree, or a strategic landmine buried in the sandy verge. I make bets with Butch and Rabbit.

Landmines are still unthinkable to me. I am betting on the tree.

In this way, we weave our way to the border, and once we reach the hotel where we can freshen up before going through customs, we are all ready for a drink. The Beitbridge Hotel is a border fixture, built in the old colonial style. It is a solid, red-roofed edifice with white columns, lazy ceiling fans, and a verandah set with wicker chairs and tables. Typically, we do not arrive here shaking and trembling, but today we do. The other members of the convoy, sitting in comfortable chairs sipping tea or quaffing down beers, stare at us as if they're amazed that we are still alive. Dad orders tea from the smartly dressed waiter as if it had all been an uneventful trip and he has no idea why anyone should stare at us. Fortunately, as we proceed through the border into South Africa, the two pots of tea he has just quaffed has woken him up or the pills have worn off. We are never sure which it is, but the rest of the trip brings us back to normality, soothing our rattled souls.

CHAPTER 56

LEAVING THE NEST

In 1968 I complete my high school curriculum. My thoughts drift to what I want to do with the rest of my life. I bounce around from job to job while trying to make up my mind. I am thinking of nursing. My real dream is to be an artist or writer, but Dad discourages me from these choices.

"It's not easy to make a living with painting," he says one day as we walk through an art gallery in Port Elizabeth, where we are vacationing. "Your mother and I only do it as a hobby." He beckons a docent over. "Can she make a living painting?" he asks the befuddled man. He points at me. "Tell her what she can expect."

The docent gives me a sympathetic glance. "It's very hard to earn enough money with painting," he says. "But don't let that discourage you." It does, though. All ideas of painting for a living vanish in a puff of smoke, and I begin to look elsewhere.

Mom has entrepreneurial friends, and one of them just opened up a hair salon. I briefly work at the salon as an untrained assistant who washes hair. I love the job. I get to meet some interesting people, and while my salary is minuscule, I pay Mom board and lodging. I am happy to do so. I feel grownup and productive.

By this time, my family has moved once again, this time to the town of Chiredzi. The house is beautiful and sits on a hill overlooking the town. Our Hippo Valley home had been lovely, too, but this house is a dream, with its bougainvillea arbors and modern design.

I am blessed, happy in my work, overjoyed with our new home, and finding new friends for a while. But it can't be long before the other shoe drops. Our capable and talented hairdresser has left, and another fills her place; a woman who not only appears uninspired, judging by her ratty hair, but whose goal seems to be to make everyone in town look just like her. Clients drop off until we are left with only one or two walk-ins per day. Mom's friend has no choice. We close. I scour the local newspaper and find a position as a clerk at a paint/hardware store.

I quickly decide this job is not what I want to do for the rest of my life. It pays more, but I dislike my boss. She reminds me of one of my junior school teachers, perhaps Miss Thorne. She is impatient with my inexperience and poor typing skills, and I am bored with the job. Inventorying cans of paint, hardware supplies, and typing letters to vendors is not my idea of being a grownup. I cannot verbalize what I expect from life as an adult, but it surely isn't this. After what feels like the billionth time my boss chastises me for a careless mistake, I decide the grass might be greener elsewhere.

I quit the hardware store. Another vacancy has opened up in town, and it is working for the mayor as his secretary. I am so excited I forget why I left my previous job: I can't type well. I apply for the job anyway. To my shock, I get it, and I am overjoyed. Yes! I think, now I can show my real stuff...what I am made of, with a higher position and more money.

Dad is not happy with the news, and pops my bubble almost immediately. "I know this man," he tells me. "He's desperate. He has gone through twenty-plus secretaries in one year. He has a reputation." I know Dad has had some terrible rows with this man in the past. They have almost come to blows, but I also think Dad isn't the easiest person to get along with, either; indeed, I am a pleasant person who will have no problem, blah blah blah. I convince myself I am doing the right thing.

The mayor is a hefty man in his fifties with a handlebar mustache. Pompous and irascible, he embodies the character of Colonel Blimp. Even though he is no longer in the British Army, he insists upon being addressed as *Colonel*. If he had been in the navy instead, they could have used him as a foghorn. His voice bellows through the halls of our offices on the second floor. His wife, Fiona, works down the hall in the accounting department. When he wants her, instead of picking up the phone or sending me to summon her, he yells, "Fiona!" His stentorian voice reverberates down the hall, and like an Olympic sprinter, Fiona runs to do his bidding.

The first three months go well enough. I put up with the Colonel's two foul-smelling dogs he brings into the office with him each day. These aren't well dogs. They are aged and flatulent. The redolence lingers, and I hold my breath every time I walk into his office. To make things worse, I am still a terrible typist. We use an old manual typewriter, and I must always type up letters and documents with umpteen carbon paper copies. Every time I make a mistake, which is frequently, I need to erase every copy, creating an untidy mess. I've never learned shorthand, so I must decipher the Colonel's spidery notes he makes on the backs of envelopes. Often, I get it wrong. The Colonel's patience runs out, and after a yelling match that brings Fiona running, so do I. Right out the door, never to return.

I am secretary number twenty-five to walk out.

EPILOGUE

Running out of the Colonel's office is the first adult decision I make. I turn my teenage face toward adulthood, blissfully ignorant, with no clue what still lies ahead for me. I am invincible, optimistic for my future. I feel like a rubber ball rebounding after each setback — malaria, bilharzia, Miss Nettles, boarding school, Colonel Blimp, and not the least of it, the dangers of the bushveld. *I am a survivor*, I think, and life tends to get better in my short experience, not worse.

How wrong I am.

The wild child years, the lessons of the walking wounded...all have shown me just how resilient I am and how much I can learn from others' misfortunes and mistakes.

Wrong, again.

Life raises an eyebrow at the unseasoned nineteen-year-old kid, knowing it will yet upend everything I think about myself, my beliefs, and my experience. However, life has been generous, too, giving me many more chapters to add. *After all*, it says, *didn't I once wish for things to be more interesting?* My wish is granted, but not in the way I expect.

Stay tuned.

THE END

REVIEWS

"Viewing a fascinating world through a child's eyes...It tells a tale of a unique childhood with sensitivity and humor."

5-Stars, Amazon Reader

"*Tea, Scones, and Malaria* is a must-read book for anyone interested in Africa...and how the southern part of that continent grew, sometimes painfully, into independence from its colonial past."

5-Stars, T. Kuch, Author

"Smooth, easy read!" A very timely book."

5-Stars, Amazon Reader

"I so enjoyed this sojourn into Africa's little-known places and people."

5-Stars, Amazon Reader

ABOUT THE AUTHOR

Katlynn Brooke is also the author of the young adult fantasy fiction *The Ialana Series*.

She currently resides in the U.S. (Virginia) and is spending her time writing even more books. She is working on a sequel to her memoir that explores her travels to exotic foreign places, talks about her battle with addiction, and offers an exciting look at the Bush War years as Rhodesia makes its final transition into the country of Zimbabwe.

Manufactured by Amazon.ca
Bolton, ON